Zacharias Tanee Fomum

Moving God
Through prayer

Éditions du Livre Chrétien
4, rue du Révérend Père Cloarec
92400 Courbevoie France
editionlivrechretien@gmail.com

Published by

EDITIONS DU LIVRE CHRÉTIEN

4, rue du Révérend Père Cloarec

92400 Courbevoie - FRANCE

Tél : (33) 9 52 29 27 72

Email : editionlivrechretien@gmail.com

I LOVINGLY DEDICATE THIS BOOK, WITH GREAT EXPECTATIONS, TO EMMANUEL BAYIHA MY FRIEND, HELPER AND MINISTER

.

Table des matières

Introduction **11**

Some thoughts on prayer 12

What is prayer ? 16

The necessity of receiving the will of God **29**

God's thoughts and God's way's 26

The example of king David 35

The example of Moses 46

The example of the Lord Jesus Christ 52

Earth governed by heaven 62

God's will in man's personal needs 65

The dangers of the permissive will of God 74

The will of God that is already known 78

Spiritual maturity and knowing the will of God 83

The desires of the heart 88

Receiving the will of God and spiritual enlargement 92

Receiving the will of God and spiritual sensitivity 95

Receiving the will of God and a spiritual walk 98

Purity of heart and the reception of the will of God 101

God the dwelling place of man 102

Man the dwelling place of God 106

Communion between God and man 111

God dwells in the believer's spirit 115

Engraving the image ....

Between revelation and asking 123

Concretizing what has been received 126

Believing what has been revealed 131

Change or transformation of heart 135

Believing that God is committed to his will 138

Believing that God will answer prayer 141

Burden : what it is 144

Faith and burden 149

Faith, burden, prayer and the goal of life 152

The development of burden 155

The discharge of burden 163

General issues - 1 164

General issues - 2 168

A heart touched 170

A heart hardened 172

A heart willing 176

A heart moved or stirred 180

A heart aglow 189

Long-term goals and long-term burdens 193

A heart aflame 197

WIth words known 203

With words unknown 208

With sighs and groans 214

Rending heaven - 1 : God doing it 223

Rending heaven - 2 : Man doing it 226

Conflict with the enemy 230

No more burden 232

Very important 244

About the author 248

Preface

This book, *"Moving God Through Prayer "* is the sixth, in the series.

The books in the series that are already written are :

1. The Way of Victorious Praying
2. The Ministry of Fasting
3. The Art of Intercession
4. The Practice of Intercession
5. With Christ in the School and Ministry of Praying
6. Moving God Through Prayer
7. Practical Spiritual Warfare through Prayer
8. The Ministry of Praise and Thanksgiving
9. Waiting on God In Prayer

The first five books have been published in hardcover by Vantage Press, 516 West 34TH Street, New York 10001, USA.

The sixth book in the series is in your hands. May the Lord bless you abundantly as you read it and may He lead you into a deeper experience with Himself. May He open your eyes to see what prayer is and then enable you to pray without ceasing.

If you have been blessed through reading this book, please enable some others to obtain the book, read it and be blessed also.

Zacharias TANEE FOMUM

P.O.BOX 6090,

Yaounde, Cameroon.

Part 1

INTRODUCTION

1
• • • • • • • •

Some thoughts on prayer

1. The first prerequisite in prayer is that a person should seek and know God's will about the issue at hand.

2. To ask God to do things that are assuredly not this will is to wage war, through prayer against God and against oneself.

3. To pray that God will put aside this will and do something else, is to attempt to murder God.

4. To pray that God would act according to the desires of one's heart instead of acting according to His pre-determined purpose is to attempt to overthrow Him; it is also to do one's spirit, soul and body untold harm.

5. Those who have begun to know God will prefer to spend ten hours praying for a revelation of God's will, than to invest ten thousand hours praying about something in which God's will is not known.

6. Those who have made spiritual progress in the knowledge of God knows that prayer is as dangerous and harmful as it is a blessing. They know that those who pray prayers that are contrary to God's will, are inviting great disaster for themselves, and it will come.

7. Those who know God's will dare not stop praying until they have seen it pass into fulfilment.

8. God's co-workers execute His will primarily through prayer.

9. One man who walks in purity and holiness and prays for three hours each day, does far more good to the kingdom of God than thousands of prayerless preachers who preach many sermons to thousands of people each day.

10. The man who prays five hours each day and reads the Bible for two hours a day then preaches, counsels, or writes for one hour a day is truly doing *"full"* time work as a servant of God, whereas the person who preaches for seven hours a day, reads the Bible for thirty minutes and prays for thirty minutes, is a spiritual spy.

11. At the judgment seat of Christ, the greatest crowns will be won by those who soaked their ministry in prayer. Such are now putting more time into praying every activity through, than the time that the activity actually takes. They have learnt that what is not done through prayer is not done at all.

12. To pray effectively we must want what God wants - that and only that is to pray in the will of God (A.W. Tozer).

13. Only long, continued, faith-filled travailing prayer can bring true revival to the church.

14. Only long, continued, faith-filled travailing prayer can bring true revival to an individual heart.

15. *"I appeal to you, brethren, by our Lord Jesus Christ and by the love of the Spirit, to strive together with me in your prayers to God on my behalf, that I may be delivered from the unbelievers in Judea, and that my service for Jerusalem may be acceptable to the saints"* (Romans 15:30-31).

16. *"You also must help us by prayer, so that many will give thanks on our behalf for the blessing granted us in answer to many prayers"* (2 Corinthians 1:11).

17. *"Do you not know that in a race all the runners compete, but only one receives the prize? So run that you may obtain it. Every athlete exercises self-control in all things"* (1 Corinthians 9:24-25). Everyone who wants to make progress in the School of Prayer must exercise self-control in everything - sleep, the use of time, the use of his mind, the use of his mouth, and so on. Without such discipline he will know only limited power in prayer because, careless thoughts and careless words result in spiritual leak.

18. *"When Daniel knew that the document had been signed, he went to his house where he had windows in his upper chamber open toward Jerusalem; and he got down upon his knees three times a day and prayed and gave thanks before his God, as he had done previously"* (Daniel 6:10).

19. *"But seek the welfare of the city where I have sent you into exile, and pray to the Lord on its behalf, for in its welfare you will find your welfare"* (Jeremiah 29:7).

20. *"There is none that calls upon thy name, that bestirs himself to take hold of thee..."* (Isaiah 64:7).

21. The Church would be better prepared for her Lord, and prepared the sooner, if all her leaders took one year off preaching and gave it entirely to seeking, through prayer and daily waiting on God, that holiness without which no man shall see God

22. All revival that is not rooted in heart-searching and heart-rending prayer to the Lord is at best human emotionalism.

23. The wisest people are students in the School of Prayer.

24. The Lord has called the wise to pray. Only fools do not obey.

25. Today is the day of prayer.

26. This year I will devote the first week-end of every month to prayer.

27. This year convert every public holiday into a praying day, spend twelve hours that day in prayer, and you will soon see a difference in your life.

28. Pray without ceasing!

29. Watch and pray!

Amen.

2
●●●●●●●●

What is prayer?

If people are to pray as they should, both in quality and in quantity, then it becomes important that they understand what prayer is. Many people will say, *"Prayer is talking to God,"* others will say, *"Prayer is asking and receiving from God."* These definitions are not wrong. There is truth in them. However, they are childish definitions that lead to childish prayers or they are partial definitions that touch on secondary and not the primary issues of prayer. The problem with the above definitions is that they put man at the centre of prayer; they exalt the needs of man; they make as if prayer was created by God to meet the needs of man as the fundamental issue. This is not true. Prayer was created by God primarily to meet the needs of God and only secondarily to meet the needs of man. Because prayer was instituted first of all to need the needs of God, mature praying focuses primarily on the needs of God and only secondarily on the needs of man.

What the lord Jesus taught

The Lord Jesus taught the disciples to pray like this:

"Our Father who art in heaven, Hallowed be thy name. Thy kingdom come, Thy will be done, on earth as it is in heaven. Give us this day our daily bread; And forgive us our debts, as we also have forgiven our debtors; And led us not into temptation, But deliver us from evil" (Matthew 6 : 9-13).

The prayer can be divided into:

1. The needs of God :
   a. Hallowed be Thy name.
   b. Thy kingdom come.
   c. Thy will be done.
2. The needs of man :
   a. Our daily bread.
   b. Our debts.
   c. Our temptations.

The Lord Jesus showed that the priority was the needs of God. That is why the first three issues are Thy, Thy, Thy. In fact, it is only when one has finished with the needs of God, that the praying person should come to the needs of man - our, our, our.

The truth is that there are believers who have never seen that God has needs. They have, therefore, never bothered about the needs of God. There are others who, although seeing that God has needs, are nevertheless so preoccupied with the needs of man that only a little time is given to the needs of God.

I think the maturity of believers can be easily deduced from what their pre-occupations in prayer are. The most mature believers are pre-occupied with the needs of God. The next class in maturity is pre-occupied with the needs of others, both those of believers and those of unbelievers. The third class in maturity is pre-occupied with personal needs.

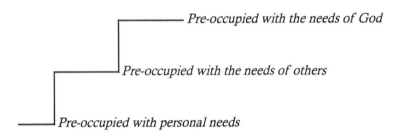

The relationship between maturity and pre-occupation in prayer

This is easily understood in the light of the fact that the more a person matures the more he is possessed by the Lord. Since one prays more readily on that which possesses one, those who are the most possessed by the Lord will pray more about the Lord's needs and those who are possessed more by self will pray more about their personal needs.

PRAYER BEGINS IN THE HEART OF GOD

Every true prayer ought to begin in the heart of God. God knows everything and God can do everything. There is a sense in which God can completely do without man. He can also supply His own needs and the needs of man without the prayers of man. Even though He can do that, He has ordained to act differently. God in His wondrous love for man has raised man to the level of a co-worker. The Bible says, *"Working together with him, then, we entreat you not to accept the grace of God in vain"* (2 Corinthians 6 : 1); *"For we are God's fellow workers; you are God's field, God's building"* (1 Corinthians 3:9).

Maybe we can illustrate the whole issue from the point of a business partnership. Suppose I am a businessman with much money with which to carry out a business. Suppose that my son Paul has no money but I decide to make him a partner in the business and to make him an obligatory co-signatory on the cheques of the business. From the time that the decisions are taken and legalized, even though Paul contributed nothing to business and I contributed everything, I cannot sign any cheques and have them honoured without that he counter signs them. I have raised him to that position but by so raising him, I have placed limitations on myself. I may no longer move at my pace in taking decisions and executing them. In fact we will have to go at his pace.

Although this illustration is not perfect, it shows something of the implications of man being a co-worker with God. The plain truth is that because God has made us His co-workers there are something that He can no longer do unless we pray. Let us just quote one example from the word. The Lord says in His word, *"The people of the land have practiced extortion and committed robbery; they have oppressed the poor and needy, and have extorted from the sojourner without redress. And I sought for a man among them who should build up the wall and stand in the breach before me for the land, that I should not destroy it; but I found none. Therefore I have poured out my indignation upon them; I have have consumed them with the fire of my wrath; their way have I requited upon their heads, says the Lord God"* (Ezekiel 22:29-31).

It is obvious that God wanted to requite this people, even though they had sinned. He needed to have just one man who would co-operate and co-work with Him by standing in the gap in prayer on their behalf. If He had found such a person He would have rejoiced and pardoned the people. Because He did not find such a person He went ahead and poured out His indignation on the people and consumed them with the fire of His wrath. We can say that those people were punished, but not just because they had sinned. They were punished because although they had sinned, there was none amongst them who would stand in the gap on their behalf before God and intercede.

God must have co-workers not only in prayer but also in other things. He is willing, nay, anxious to save sinners. Jesus has died for them and sent the Holy Spirit to convince, convict and convert them. However, God must have man who is His co-worker prevent the message of salvation to the lost. Unless God's co-worker does that, God's great desire and His great work in salvation is more or less put to nought. We cannot run away from this. It makes man important, critically important, in the accomplishments of the programmes of God. That is what partnership demands and God has accepted it.

THE SOVEREIGNTY OF MAN

By choosing to have man as His co-worker, God has made man to be sovereign. Man is sovereign within the sovereignty of God. Man has limited sovereignty within the limitless sovereignty of God. Although man's sovereignty is limited, it is nevertheless far-reaching. Man can choose where he would spend eternity. If he chooses to reject the love of God and the wooing of the Holy Spirit, he will have his way and perish. The believer also has sovereignty in determining whether or not people will hear the gospel, and consequently, be saved. Jesus told the disciples, *"If you forgive the sins of any, they are forgiven; if you retain the sins of any, they are retained"* (John 20:23).

So, although God is God, He has exalted His co-worker to a position of sovereignty. That sovereignty is even more obvious in prayer.

What then is prayer?

Prayer involves the seeking, knowing and praying through that which is on God's heart so that He may act upon it. A praying man first seeks to know what God's need is, i.e., what is on God's heart or what His will is in a certain situation. He will allow that which he knows to possess his being in such a way that he yearns to see it happen, not just because it is God's will but also because it has become the very desire of his heart. What was on God's heart is now on man's heart. What was the desire of God has now become the desire of man and what was the will of God has now become the will of man. Man then prays this matter that originated in God's heart back to God. He labours in prayer to ensure that what gets back to God is what was there initially. When that which started in God's heart gets back to God as the *"will"* of His co-worker, God's heart is satisfied, and He moves to execute His will, which is also the *"will"* of His co-worker. In that way God is satisfying His heart and the heart of His co-worker. Both have been involved and when the answer comes, both are fulfilled. We can illustrate it as follows:

Part 2

THE NECESSITY OF RECEIVING THE WILL OF GOD

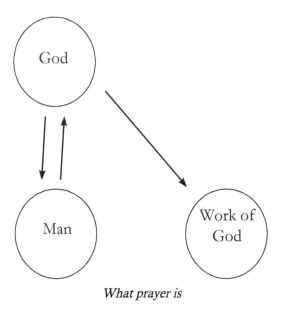

What prayer is

Mature believers are pre-occupied with God. They are secondarily pre-occupied with the needs of God. Thirdly they are pre-occupied with the needs of other people. Lastly they are pre-occupied with their own needs. Because it needs the revelation of God before a man can truly know God, know God's needs, know the needs of others and know one's own needs, mature believers spend much time before God not so much in asking that He does things but that He reveals Himself and His will to them. This will include His needs, the needs of others and the needs of the praying person. Once the needs are known, the person can then begin to plead that the Lord should grant them.

It may seem ridiculous to some, that a person should plead with God to reveal His needs to him so that he should plead with Him to grant them. However, for the one who has learnt to know God and to walk before Him, this is actually the greatest thing that can happen to him - that God should reveal His need to him and thus give him the privilege of begging Him in prayer to fulfil His need. I was told of a tribe in Western Uganda that had very rich kings. The kings were so rich and so loved that subjects came and knelt with their gifts, pleading that the king might do them the undeserved favour of receiving a gift from them. They were begging to give. If they begged to give to man and found great pleasure and fulfilment in having their gifts received how much more should the sons of the King of kings find utmost pleasure in seeking, knowing and begging God for the favour of meeting His needs?

3
• • • • • • • •

God's thoughts and God's ways

"For my thoughts are not your thoughts, neither are your ways my ways, says the Lord. For as the heavens are higher than the earth, so are my ways higher than your ways and my thoughts than your thoughts. For as the rain and the snow come down from heaven, and return not thither but water the earth, making it bring forth and sprout, giving seed to the sower and bread to the eater, so shall my word be that goes forth from my mouth; it shall not return to me empty, but it shall accomplish that which I purpose, and prosper in the thing for which I sent it. For you shall go out in joy, and be led forth in peace; the mountains and the hills before you shall break forth into singing, and all the trees of the field shall clap their hands. Instead of the thorn shall come up the cypress; instead of the brier shall come up the myrtle; and it shall be to the Lord for a memorial, for an everlasting sign which shall not be cut off" (Isaiah 55:8-13).

GOD'S VERDICT

The Lord said, *"My thoughts are not your thoughts."* The Lord still says, *"My thoughts are not your thoughts."* That is the verdict of God. He continued, *"My ways are not your ways."* That again is the verdict of God.

The question is, *"Do you believe that God's thoughts are not your thoughts and that His ways are not your ways?"* I want to be honest and admit that I have not always believed this. The evidence of this is the fact that I have dared to think my own thoughts and make my own decisions and even gone ahead to execute them. Or I have thought my own thoughts and made my own plans and brought them to God for approval. I have had my own way of doing things and even done them that way, without immediately realising that I was doing great harm to myself and even worse, frustrating the purposes of God. It is only recently that the Lord has brought me to face these things squarely.

The Lord says that as the heavens are higher than the earth, so are His ways higher than the ways of man and His thoughts higher than the thoughts of man. This is frightful! God is actually saying that the difference between His thoughts and the thoughts of man and between His ways and the ways of man, are like the difference between heaven and earth! This means that there is no place whatsoever for the thoughts and the ways of man to stand before God.

The thoughts of men are not all alike. There are varying degrees of correctness of men's thoughts. There are also varying degrees of correctness of human ways. There are those whose thoughts and ways are good. There are others whose thoughts and ways are better. There are yet others whose thoughts and ways are the best. We can illustrate the difference in the thoughts and ways of men as follows:

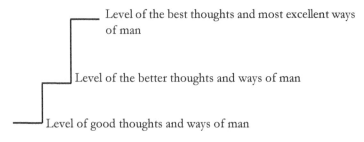

Level of the best thoughts and most excellent ways of man

Level of the better thoughts and ways of man

Level of good thoughts and ways of man

Level of good thoughts and ways of man

VARYING PLANES OF HUMAN THOUGHTS AND WAYS.

We can say that the man with good thoughts and good ways is above others. His good thoughts and ways are at roof level, compared to the thoughts and ways of the masses. We can also say that the man with better thoughts and ways has his thoughts and ways at the level of a high hill. Finally, we can say that the one with the best thoughts and the best ways has his thoughts at the height of a very high mountain. However the thoughts and the ways of God are at the heights of heaven. We can illustrate this as follows:

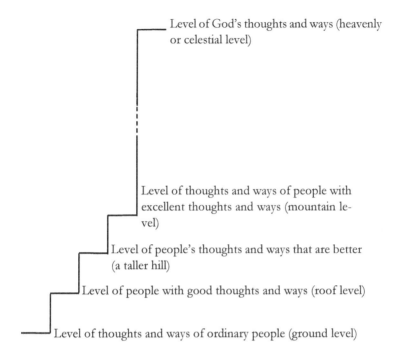

Level of God's thoughts and ways (heavenly or celestial level)

Level of thoughts and ways of people with excellent thoughts and ways (mountain level)

Level of people's thoughts and ways that are better (a taller hill)

Level of people with good thoughts and ways (roof level)

Level of thoughts and ways of ordinary people (ground level)

It is immediately obvious that the persons on the roof, high hill or mountain top can only boast about their thoughts and their ways if they do not look at the heavens. If they dare to look at the heavens they will immediately acknowledge that their best thoughts and their best ways are utter foolishness by comparison. They would not ask anyone to think like them. They would not ask anyone to be guided by their thoughts and their ways. They will forsake their ways and plead with everyone not to imitate them but to seek the thoughts of God and know them.

Although God has made the proclamation and although the logic of it is very evident, the Enemy has blinded the world and even blinded the children of the kingdom, so much that they are pursuing their own thoughts and their own ways or they are pursuing the best thoughts and the best ways of the best men and thereby hoping to please God.

We state conclusively that even the best thoughts of the most obedient child of God are still the thoughts of men. We insist that the best that originates in man is very far removed from the thoughts and the ways of God. We proclaim that the most *"foolish"* thought of God is as far greater and better than the best thought of the lost spiritual man, as the heavens are higher than the earth.

This means that for the person who wants to pray, there is no substitute for seeking the will of God. Such a one must put aside his thoughts and ways. He must forsake the thoughts and the ways of man and he must come to the Lord and seek, find and know the will of God. It is upon knowing the will of God that he can begin to really pray.

PRELIMINARY PRAYERS

Since the thoughts and ways of God are higher than the highest and best thoughts of the best men even as the heavens are higher than the highest mountain top, it is imperative that the first part of the prayers of any who would make progress be spent in seeking God's will. At that stage in prayer, the believer has the liberty to ask the Lord to show him His will and His ways.

Moses prayed to the Lord, saying, *"Now therefore, I pray thee, if I have found favour in thy sight, show me now thy ways, that I may know thee and find favour in thy sight"* (Exodus 33:13). He did not pray in vain; for the Bible says, *"He made known his ways to*

Moses" (Psalm 103:7). Moses prayed that the Lord might show him His ways. The Lord answered that prayer. When the Lord showed Moses His ways, Moses could then pray that the Lord might enable him to walk in those ways.

It is interesting that Moses, who had walked so intimately with God and seen God's power manifested in Egypt, at the Red Sea and in the wilderness still needed to know God's ways. He knew God and know himself. He knew the difference between God's ways and his own ways. He then laboured to ensure that he sought and knew God's ways in everything. His was a constant cry to the Lord that His ways might be shown to him. He did not presume that because he knew God's ways about some matter, he necessarily knew God's will about other issues. He did not presume that because he had known God's will in the past, he necessarily knew God's will in the present. He therefore sought the Lord unceasingly and because of that he knew God's ways continuously.

It is therefore important that the sincere believer decides to seek God's will about every issue before he begins to pray intensely about it. Take, for example, that there is a desire in the heart to travel to some country. The fact that there is a desire in the heart does not necessarily mean that it is God's will that the journey be made. There may even be an invitation to come to that country and perform some important duty. In addition, funds may be available to cover all the expenses of the trip. Does all this mean that God has necessarily ordained that the trip to be made? Certainly not. All the external factors may cohere about something in particular, yet the Lord may be uninterested in it. On the other hand the outward circumstances may all be negative - no invitation, no money and so forth; yet God's will may be that the trip be made. So, when the

invitation comes, the will of God should still be sought. The
praying saint should go to his heavenly Father and spread the
invitation before Him and also place the ticket before the Lord.
He should then pray, saying, "Lord, this invitation has come to
me. The resources that will make it easy for it to be honoured
are available and are here before You. O Lord, I do not know
what Your will is. I cannot trust the desire of my heart because
it may not be the desire of Your heart. I could go astray, O
Lord. Therefore, Lord, show Your servant Your way about this
matter and give him the grace to walk in it. The Lord's answer
will come to his waiting servant. It may come during the first
prayer session on the matter or it may come during subsequent
prayer sessions. It may even come when the believer is not
praying. One thing we know for certain is that the will of the
Lord will come to those who desire to know it.

If the believer receives from the Lord that he should make
the trip, he should then begin to pray about the details of the
trip and should orientate his entire personality in the direction
of doing God's will by going on the trip. If on the other hand
the believer, while he seeks God's will about the matter comes
to a knowledge that the Lord does not want him to go on
the journey, he must refuse to go, return the ticket and all the
other advantages that could come with the trip. It must be
abandoned. This is the way to walk in the thoughts and the
ways of God.

SEEKING THE WILL OF GOD

We have shown that the will of God must be sought. The
men of God sought God's will. The Bible encourages all God's
children to seek His will. A few references will drive home the

point. The Psalmist prayed, saying, *"Make me to know thy ways, O Lord; teach me thy paths"* (Psalm 25:4). He continued to cry out to God, saying, *"Teach me thy way, O Lord; and lead me on a level path because of my enemies"* (Psalm 27:11).

The Lord has promised to reveal His will to those who seek Him. He says, *"I will instruct you and teach you the way you should go; I will counsel you with my eye upon you"* (Psalm 32:8).

Settle it for ever that you will find out God's will about everything before you begin to pray. Decide that even under the pressure of circumstances you will still turn to the Lord and seek His will, know it and then pray accordingly.

ASSURANCE

When an individual has sought God's will and known it, he can then apply himself to bold and violent praying. Such a one now knows that the will of God, which he knows, must be done. He will leave no stone unturned in prayer to ensure that he presses through in prayer until the answer comes. He will wrestle with each and every obstacle that the Enemy may put in the way of his prayers. He will have no time to add, *"if it is Your will O Lord."* He knows that it is God's will and that God's will must be done. This will lead to tenacity, aggression, wrestling, and all that it will take to have God's answer. He will not only pray, he will do everything that he can to ensure that he cooperates with God so that the answer comes.

All this is possible to the person who has sorted out God's ways from his ways and God's through from his thoughts. Having sorted things out he has decided to put his thoughts and his ways away and to take God's thoughts and God's ways as the only legitimate ones for him.

A PERSONAL QUESTION

Are there things that you are taking up with God in prayer about which you have not sought His will? If there are such things you should immediately stop praying about them until you have come to a knowledge of God's will about them.

To continue to insist that God should do something that is not His will is to sin gravely. To continue to insist that God should do something about which we have no assurance is also to sin. It is to tempt God. It is not enough to say that I will pray and leave things to God so that He should sort them out and answer those prayers that are according to His will and leave the rest.

Such an attitude is wrong for several reasons. First of all, it is the shifting to God of a responsibility that is the believer's. He has ordained that He will do what He must do and leave to the believer what the believer must do. It is the believer's duty (and not God's) to find out what God's will about issue is, before requests are made to God for action. The second reason is that it is more difficult to pray and continue to pray on an issue over which the will of God is not known. Deep burdens come with a knowledge of the fact that something is God's will and being God's will, it is a must that it be done. The third reason is that God may grant us the desires of our hearts that are not His perfect will, as judgment on us. Can anyone afford to take such a risk? Are you taking such a risk?

4

· · · · · · · · ·

The example of king David

"Now when David dwelt in his house, David said to Nathan the prophet," Behold I dwell in a house of cedar, but the ark of the covenant of the Lord is under a tent. "And Nathan said to David," Do all that is in your heart, for God is with you. "But the same night the word of the Lord came to Nathan," Go and tell my servant David, "Thus says the Lord: You shall not build me a house to dwell in. For I have not dwelt in a house since the day I led up Israel to this day, but I have gone from tent to tent and from dwelling to dwelling. In all places where I have moved with all Israel, did I speak a word with any of the judges of Israel, whom I commanded to shepherd my people saying," Why have you not built me a house of cedar? "Now therefore thus shall you say to my servant David," Thus says the Lord of hosts, I took you from the pasture, from following sheep, that you should be a prince over my people Israel; and I have been with you wherever you went, and have cut off all your enemies from before you; and I will make for you a name, like the name of the great ones of the earth. And I will appoint a place for my people Israel, and will plant them, that they may dwell in their own place, and be disturbed no more; and violent men shall waste them no more, as formerly, from the time that I appointed judges over my people Israel; and I will subdue all your enemies. Moreover I declare to you that the Lord will build you a house. When your days are fulfilled to go to be with your fathers, I will raise up your offspring after you, one of your own sons, and I will establish his kingdom. He shall build a house for *me, and I will establish his throne for ever. I will be his father, and he shall be my son; I will not take my steadfast love from him, as I look it from him who was before you, but I will confirm him in my house and in my kingdom for ever and his throne shall be establish for ever.'* *"In accordance with all these words, and in accordance with all this vision, Nathan spoke to David"* (I Chronicles 17:1-15).

THE GOOD THOUGHTS OF KING DAVID

David loved the Lord. He was very sensitive in his spirit. He had built a house of cedar for himself and as he looked around, he was touched by the fact that the ark of the covenant of the Lord was under a tent. He thought this was not right and decided that things ought to be done to give the ark of the covenant of the Lord a better dwelling place. He thought he should build a dwelling place for the ark of the covenant of the Lord.

Having had such thoughts, he did not start executing them without consultation. He consulted Nathan the prophet. When Nathan heard the thoughts of David, they occurred to him to be most correct. There was nothing selfish in them. There was going to be much sacrifice involved on the part of king David and there was no selfish motive involved. It was obvious that all the glory for the project would go to the Lord. Nathan was so convinced about the rightness of the project that he thought God must like it and so he encouraged David to go ahead and execute the desires of his heart.

The project originated in David's spirit. The project sounded correct to the prophet and received his approval but the project was not of God! That night God stepped in and spoke to the prophet, asking him to tell David, *"You shall not build me a house to dwell in."*

Here we see clearly that a project flowed from David's heart and was approved by a prophet who was walking with God but the project was not of God.

The good thoughts of David were wrong. The imaginations of the prophet were wrong. God's will was different.

SEEKING MAN INSTEAD OF SEEKING GOD.

There are two problems in our day. The one problem is that of people who carry out every imagination of their hearts and believe that they have heard God or that they have been sent by Him. They believe that the voice of their spirits must be the voice of God and upon hearing such a voice, move ahead into action, believing that they are doing God's will. Such people do not know that the voice of the human spirit is not the voice of the Holy Spirit. They do not know that the voice of the human spirit is of necessity wrong, unless the human spirit has received its message from the Holy Spirit.

The Holy Spirit imparts the will of God to the human spirit---The will of God comes through the human spirit and is received by the human mind.

The human spirit releases thoughts that originates in itself---The will of man comes through the human spirit and is received by the human mind and may be mistaken for the will of God.

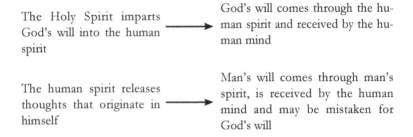

| The Holy Spirit imparts God's will into the human spirit | → | God's will comes through the human spirit and received by the human mind |
| The human spirit releases thoughts that originate in himself | → | Man's will comes through man's spirit, is received by the human mind and may be mistaken for God's will |

This situation means that a person who is led by the human spirit will certainly be wrong. Those who are correct are those who are led by the Holy Spirit. The Bible says, *"For all who are led by the Spirit of God are sons of God"* (Romans 8:14). We say that all who are led by the human spirit are sons of human beings. The believer must realise that not every movement of his spirit is in response to the move of the Holy Spirit. This knowledge will save many from much error.

The second problem is that there are believers who have come to recognize the presence of spiritual people in their midst. Those spiritual people walk in holiness before God and are totally consecrated to Him. Although these people are often and maybe most often led by the Holy Spirit, they can still be led by their spirits or by their minds. When this happens they too are led by their spirits or souls and their judgments are just as wrong. Nathan was such a man and the counsel that he gave king David was not the will of God. It did not flow from God but from him. The way to correctness about the will of God is for every believer to take upon himself the responsibility to seek the will of God in the things that concern him. He must pray and pray. He must wait before God. He must plead with God to show him His will. He must acknowledge before God that by using his reasoning or the impressions of his spirit he could be wrong. He must therefore plead for God's intervention.

He must be earnest before God, being prepared to bring the issue over and over before the Lord, pleading that the Lord would help him not to be mistaken. When he has come to the place of firm assurance before God about the matter, he must now turn to a spiritual person and seek his confirmation. This means that he would bring the matter to the spiritual person and expose the details and the conclusion that he has arrived at to him. He must then plead with the spiritual person to go and seek God about the matter. Without the willingness to allow the spiritual person time to go and seek the Lord's will in prayer, but to demand an immediate confirmation is to ask the spiritual man to give what his immediate thoughts or feelings are. This is to court the type of answer that king David received from prophet Nathan. Any spiritual person who feels that he has reached the place in spiritual maturity where the first impressions of his spirit are always the will of God is deceived, and will make many mistakes and misguide many. Every person must turn to the Lord in prayer to seek His will, having no confidence in anything that originates in himself. This will prevent many errors.

THE NEED FOR HUMILITY

The proud of heart will find it difficult to leave the will of God. They will think that they know what they do not know. They will not humble themselves before the lord to acknowledge that they might be wrong. They will not humble themselves to seek the counsel of another. They believe themselves too much to bring an issue over and over before the Lord. Because every human being is proud of heart, there is need to cry to God for the indispensable humility. God guides the humble.

Moses was the meekest person and consequently he received a lot of guidance from the Lord. The Bible says, *"He leads the humble in what is right, and teaches the humble his way"* (Psalm 25:9).

This humility means that the humble will not take anything for granted. They will not presume that because they were correct in the past they must necessarily be correct in the present situation before they have sought and known the will of God. They will like the Psalmist meditate and search their spirits (Psalm 77:6), and after that give another the opportunity to meditate and search his spirit about the same matter. In this way they will continue to cling and to cry out to God, saying, *"Teach me thy way, O Lord, that I may walk in thy truth; unite my heart to fear thy name"* (Psalm 86:11). Then they will know the will of God and walk in it.

GOD'S WAY HIGHER THAN MAN'S WAY

David had intended to build a house for the Lord. He would have invested much into that project for many years. The Lord knew his intentions and sent word to him, saying, *"You shall not build me a house to dwell in"* If the Lord had ended there, it would have been easy to understand. However, the Lord did not end there. He went on to say to David. *"Moreover I declare to you that the Lord will build you a house."* So David passed from the condition where he would have been building a house for the Lord to the state where he was to receive a house from the Lord. We can illustrate it as follows:

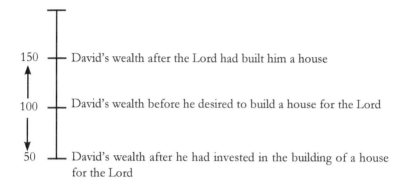

150 — David's wealth after the Lord had built him a house

100 — David's wealth before he desired to build a house for the Lord

50 — David's wealth after he had invested in the building of a house for the Lord

David's wealth to show that God's ways are not man's ways; that God's ways are higher than man's ways, even if God had only built David a house of cedar.

According to David's best thoughts, he was to do something for God. He was to build a house for the Lord. David was to give. According to God's ways, David was not only just to keep what he had by not building a house for the Lord but much more, David was to have a house built for him by the Lord. It is indeed great. That instead of pouring yourself to build a house for the Lord, you are doubly blessed, not only to keep that which you intended to give but to have an additional gift, you have entered into the dimensions of God, for He always gives exceedingly abundantly more than we intend to give to Him.

PHYSICAL HOUSE OR SPIRITUAL HOUSE

The difference was not only in the fact that David, instead of building a house for the Lord received a house from the Lord. The difference even extends in the type of house that he wanted to build and the type of house that he received. David had intended to build a house of cedar for the Lord. The

Lord liberated him from that charged and instead took upon
Himself to build David a house. However, the house that the
Lord gave David was not one of cedar, like what David had in
mind. It was more than a house. It was a lineage; it was a house
of kings beginning with David and ending in David's greater
son - the Lord Jesus Christ. So David offered to build the lord a
physical house of cedar. God instead offered David something
far greater than a house; God offered him something that went
beyond man; God offered him an eternal throne with the Lord
Jesus who is the King of kings as a part of David's heritage.
Looked upon in this way, there is no comparison whatsoever
between what David was offering and what he received. We
can then put it as illustrated below:

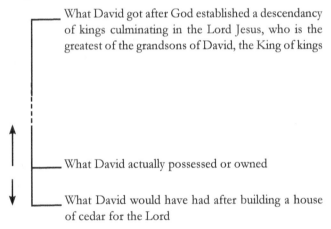

What David got after God established a descendancy
of kings culminating in the Lord Jesus, who is the
greatest of the grandsons of David, the King of kings

What David actually possessed or owned

What David would have had after building a house
of cedar for the Lord

*The incomparable greatness between God's ways
and man's ways*

I have never ceased to be amazed by the fact that unceasingly
God's ways are higher than man's ways as the heavens are higher
than the earth. Let me bring one more example from Scripture.
David sinned with Bathsheba and repented. Man's way would
have meant that the children from the later marriage between

David and Bathsheba would have been barely tolerable to the Lord. This would have been man's way of thinking and reacting. However, we see something else in the Word. The Bible says, *"Then David comforted his wife, Bathsheba, and went in to her, and lay with her; and she bore a son, and he called his name Solomon. And the Lord loved him, and sent a message by Nathan the prophet; so he called his name Jedidiah (that is, beloved of the Lord), because of the Lord"* (2 Samuel 12:24-25). So this one who could barely have been tolerated became beloved of the Lord, according to God and not according to man. Again the Lord did not only love Solomon in a special way. He went beyond that. He appointed him to be the next king after David. The Bible says, *"David said to Solomon, 'My son, I had it in my heart to build a house to the name of the Lord my God. But the word of the Lord came to me, saying, 'You have shed much blood and have waged great wars; you shall not build a house to my name, because you have shed so much blood before me upon the earth. Behold, a son shall be born to you; he shall be a man of peace. I will give him peace from all his enemies round about; for his name shall be. Solomon, and I will give peace and quiet to Israel in his days. He shall build a house for my name. He shall be my son, and I will be his father, and I will establish his royal throne in Israel for ever'"* (1 Chronicles 22:7-10). Only the Lord, the God of heaven could have done this. He is great. He deserves total worship. Let us worship Him.

I believe that it is now very evident that God's ways are radically different from man's ways. I hope it is most obvious to you that God's ways are radically different from yours. I hope you do not need further convincing to see and to forever know that God's ways are not yours and that His will is not yours. If you have truly perceived this then there is only one way by which you can manifest the fact that you have seen. It is by putting aside your thoughts in everything and putting aside your will in everything (and diligently seeking God's will and God's way in everything. If you have indeed seen that God's ways and thoughts are heavenly and your best ways and best will is earthly, you will truly abhor your own ways and your own will and put them aside in everything) without the slightest sympathy. You will decide never to do anything according to your own way regardless of what promising results may be in view. Rather, you would decide to seek God and seek God's ways, regardless of what it may cost you; pursuit of God's will will mean that you will decidedly never compromise God's will and God's ways to please any man for that would be to change that which is as high as the heavens for that which is as low as the earth.

SEEKING GOD'S WILL WHOLE-HEARTEDLY

The discovery that the ways of God are better than those of man as the heavens are higher than the earth will lead those who have seen, not only to seek God's will and God's ways but to seek these whole-heartedly. For such people, the possibility of pursuing anything less than the will of God and the ways of God has been forever abandoned. For them, the will and the ways of God are not only good. They are a must. They are the only option opened to them. They will, therefore, seek the will of God diligently and whole-heartedly. For such, they would rather do nothing than do that which is not assuredly the will of God. They will follow the example of the Psalmist who testified, saying, *"Blessed are those who keep his testimonies, who seek him with their whole heart, who also do no wrong, but walk in his ways!"* (Psalm 119:2); *"I will praise thee with an upright heart, when I learn thy righteous ordinances"* (Psalm 119:7); *"With my whole heart I seek thee; let me not wander from thy commandments!"* (Psalm 119:10); *"With my whole heart I cry, answer me O Lord! I will keep thy statutes"* (Psalm 119:145).

Such whole-hearted commitment to seek the Lord and His will will mean that until they have ascertained God's mind about something, they will take no sides and make no pronouncements. It means that until they know God's will about something they will not begin to pour out their own wills and their own ways before Him in prayer, but will prayerfully seek His will until it is known. It means that once they have known God's will they will take no rest and give God no rest. They will pray night, and day and continuing without ceasing until the Lord has risen in His great might and established His will by answering their prayers.

Lord, O that the saints would heed this! Amen.

5

••••••••

The example of Moses

"And he said to Moses, 'Come up to the Lord, you and Aaron, Nadab, and Abihu, and seventy of the elders of Israel, and worship afar off. Moses shall come near to the Lord; but the others shall not come near, and the people shall not come up with him" (Exodus 24:1-2). *"Then Moses and Aaron, Nadab, and Abihu, and seventy of the elders of Israel went up, and they saw the God of Israel; and there was under his feet as it were a pavement of sapphire stone, like the very heaven for clearness. And he did not lay his hand on the chief men of the people of Israel; they beheld God, and ate and drank. The Lord said to Moses, 'Come up to me on the mountain, and wait there; and I will give you the tables of stone, with the law and the commandment, which I have written for their instruction."* So Moses rose with his servant Joshua, and Moses went up into the mountain of God. And he said to the elder, *'Tarry here for us, until we come to you again; and behold, Aaron and Hur are with you; whoever has a cause, let him go to them.'*

Then Moses went up on the mountain, and the cloud covered the mountain. The glory of the Lord settled on Mount Sinai, and the cloud covered it six days; and on the seventh day he called to Moses out of the midst of the cloud. Now the appearance of the glory of the Lord was like is devouring fire on the top of the mountain in the sight of the people of Israel.

And Moses entered the cloud, and went up on the mountain. And Moses was on the mountain forty days and forty nights.

The Lord said to Moses, *"Speak to the people of Israel, that they take for me an offering; from every man whose heart makes him willing you shall receive the offering for me. And this is the offering which you shall receive from the: gold, silver and bronze, blue and purple and scarlet staff and fine twined linen, goat's hair, tanned rams' skins, goatskins, acacia wood, oil for the lamps, spices for the anointing oil and for the fragrant incense, onyx stones, and stones for setting, for the ephod and for the breastpiece. And let them make me a sanctuary, that i may dwell in their midst. According to all that I show you concerning the pattern of the tabernacle, and all its furniture, so you shall make it"* (Exodus 24:9-25:9).

GOD'S INITIATIVE

The Lord had a burden. He wanted to dwell in the midst of the children of Israel. He decided that He would dwell in a tabernacle and also decided what the tabernacle was to be obtained. All this was settled in His heart.

The Lord then wanted co-operation from man. He decided to call Moses, Aaron, Aaron's elder sons and seventy of the elders of Israel apart. They came apart and He let them see Him. What He allowed them to see was His feet. They beheld Him (his feet) and were satisfied and fulfilled and so ate and drank.

The Lord decided to call Moses away from the rest and so He invited him, saying, *"Come up to me on the mountain and wait there; and I will give you the tables of stone, with the law and the commandment which I have written for their instruction."* Moses went up and the glory of the Lord settled on Mount Sinai and the cloud covered it six days and on the seventh day the Lord called out to Moses and Moses went into the cloud, into the immediate presence of God and was on the mountain for forty days and nights.

When Moses was taken apart, the Lord told him what was on His mind. He told him about the sanctuary that He wanted built and told him how the things for it were to be obtained. He showed Moses the pattern of the tabernacle and all its furniture. All the details were given, such that when they were written out they covered seven chapters of the Bible. Every detail was given. Nothing was left to the initiative of Moses.

It can clearly be seen that God did not give Moses some broad outlines and then leave him to fit in the details. God gave all the details. The method for obtaining the material and the type of materials were spelt out. There was no room for Moses to add or subtract.

DURATION OF STAY ON THE MOUNTAIN

Moses was not the one who decided how long he was to stay on the mountain. The duration was decided by the Lord. There was the time needed for him to prepare to enter into God's presence. I think that he needed that time to be fully tuned away from the people he led and to be fully tuned to God; Then when he went into the cloud, the length of stay was decided upon not by him but by the Lord. Even about this, the Lord did not decide arbitrarily. He did not say, *"I am calling Moses to come and spend this number of days in My presence."* He called Moses apart and began to show him the heavenly model of the tabernacle. After the model was shown, He gave him instructions about who was to serve in the tabernacle and how he was to serve. He also gave instructions about how those to serve in the tabernacle were to be dressed. He even gave details about how the clothing of the high priest and the priests were to be made. He also revealed to Moses who was to be involved in building the tabernacle, saying, *"See, I have called by name Bezalel the son of Uri, son of Hur, of the tribe of Judah; and I have filled him with the Spirit of God, with ability and intelligence, with knowledge and all craftsmanship, to devise artistic designs, to work in gold, silver and bronze, in cutting stones for setting, and in carving wood, for work in every craft. And behold, I have appointed with him Oholiab, the son of Ahisamach, of the tribe of Dan; and I have given to all able men ability, that they may make all that I have commanded you: the tent of meeting, and the ark of the testimony, and the mercy seat that is thereon, and all the furnishings of the tent, the table and its utensils, and the pure lampstand with all its utensils, and the altar of incense, and the altar of burnt offering with all its utensils, and the laver and its base, and the finely worked garments, the holy garments for Aaron the priest and the garments of his sons, for their service as priests, and the anointing oil and the fragrant incense for the holy place. According to all that I have commanded you they shall do"* (Exodus 31:2-11).

The duration of the stay on the mountain was decided by how long it took for the lord to show Moses the heavenly ordeal of the tabernacle and for all the related details to be given to him. It was decided by how fast Moses could see and understand. Probably he asked questions in order to understand. Probably he looked at aspects of the model over and over to ensure that he really saw. When all was finished, the Lord gave him the two tables of the testimony and that was the end. It had taken forty days. Moses did not decide that he would not eat. The work he was involved in, in the presence of the Lord totally pre-occupied him that there was no time nor thought for food or drink. He was God's guest and so God fed him the way He (God) feeds Himself.

There is needed in our generation people who will know God the way Moses knew him and walk with Him the way Moses walked with Him. God, did not just decide that He wanted a representative of the people. He wanted someone who could stand the six days of preparation and all the days that it took to be in God's presence. He wanted someone whose heart and all were pure enough so that he could be at home in His (God's) presence. He wanted someone who could put aside all his ideas and take God's will whole-heartedly, seeking to add nothing to it. He found Moses and so invited Moses to Himself.

If all that Israel could provide at that moment was Aaron and his sons and the people who were related to Him as the seventy elders of the people of Israel who were chosen, then God would have had to wait. He will not use just anyone. There are some tasks for which God is prepared to wait for even one hundred years before He can act. He waits and waits for the right person who can receive the revelation and pray it back to Him without adding his own ideas. When such a one appears, He moves into action. Until He appears, He must wait.

THERE IS A MODEL IN THE HEART OF GOD FOR ALL THAT HE WANTS DONE

It is my personal conviction that there is a heavenly model, a model on the heart of God; a model of His own origin, with all His details about everything that He wants to do and everything that He wants done. If His children would put aside their own ideas, plans, and schemes and humbly seek His face and wait before Him, pleading that He may reveal the heavenly model to them, He would do it. They would then labour in prayer, presenting all that He wants done to Him and insisting that He answers their prayer by bringing His will to execution, He would do it and a new day will dawn upon the Church. The question is, *"Will He find such people among His children?"* The question is, *"Are you one such person?"* The last question is, *"Are you praying that you would become such a person and that other believers in the Lord Jesus would become such people?"*

Unless such people appear on the scene and are used by God, the Church is likely to continue in this pathway of self-initiated projects and prayers for their accomplishment and miss God's best entirely. Lord, in Your love for the Church, do not let this happen. O Lord, do not let this happen. Lord, move in might and raise such men and receive the glory for it.

Amen.

6
········

The example of the Lord Jesus Christ

We are insisting that prayer should be the proclamation of the will of God. We are insisting that the one who is praying should first of all endeavour to know what the will of the Lord is and then pray that will to Him. We are insisting upon the fact that people should not come and pour out the desires of their hearts indiscriminately to God in prayer. Rather, they should first sort out which of these desires represent the will of God. Upon such sorting out, that which is the will of God should be prayed through and that which is not should be rejected and not mentioned to God at all. We are insisting that there is no room in prayer for the brilliant thoughts of men's hearts. Rather, there is place for the will of God.

THE WILL OF JESUS CHRIST

The Lord Jesus was born into this world and took upon Himself our humanity. As a man the Lord Jesus had a spirit, soul and body. The soul of Jesus was made up of His will, mind and emotion. Because the Lord did not inherit our sinful humanity and because He never fell into sin nor yielded to sin,

His will was free from bondage to self and sin. His will was always good, and was always inclined towards good. His will was always inclined to the Father.

Although the will of Jesus was always good, always inclined towards good and always inclined towards the Father, it was nevertheless not the will of God the Father but the perfect will of the Man Jesus Christ. This means (and I write humbly, knowing that I am treading on most holy ground) that there were two wills while the Lord Jesus was on earth - His and His Father's. The Lord Jesus said, *"For I have come down from heaven, not to do my own will, but the will of him who sent me; and this is the will of him who sent me, that I should lose nothing of all that he has given me, but raise it up at the last day. For this is the will of my Father, that every one who sees the Son and believes in him should have eternal life; and I will raise him up at the last day"* (John 6:38-40).

Before the Lord Jesus came to earth, His will and the Father's will were always one. Then, the will of the Father was totally inseparable from the will of the Son. In heaven, the Lord Jesus did His will which cas the same as the Father's will. In heaven, the Lord Jesus did not need to seek the Father's will. He just knew it because the Father's will was His (the Lord Jesus'). Now that the Lord Jesus is back in heaven, His will and the Father's will are indivisibly one even as they were before He came to earth.

However, when the Lord Jesus took upon Himself our humanity, He also emptied Himself of the Father's will and accepted a will that was like man's except that the will that Jesus had was not bent or twisted by sin or self. It was wholesome. It was pure. It was right. The will that the Lord Jesus had while on earth was like the unfallen will of man, not under the bondage of sin or the damage (in part or in whole) caused by the fall.

JESUS PUT ASIDE HIS WILL, SOUGHT THE FATHER'S WILL IN EVERYTHING AND DID.

The Bible says that the Lord Jesus learned obedience. What is obedience but the seeking, knowing and doing the will of God? Before a person can obey, he has to know what his will is and put it aside completely. We can say that there are two sides to obedience. On the one side there is the knowing and rejecting of the will of self and on the other there is the seeking, knowing and doing of the will of the Lord. Jesus learned obedience by daily putting aside His own will and daily doing the will of the Father. He settled it once and for all that in everything He would put aside His own will and do the will of the Father. In a sense that is what consecration is about. It is the conscious commitment to put aside ones own will in everything and to seek, know and do God's will in everything. For the consecrated person, once the will of God about any issue is known, the pathway of action is permanently settled. For the truly consecrated person, once the will of God about any matter is known there can be no rethinking as to what will be the repercussions of disobedience for such thinking testifies to the fact that the person could choose to disobey. So the Lord Jesus learned to know the Father's will and to obey it. It would be best to say that the Lord Jesus learned to seek the Father's will. I think that was the only thing that He needed since He had settled it for ever in heaven that He would obey the Father in all things and at all times. THE SCHOOL OF OBEDIENCE IS ACTUALLY THE SCHOOL OF SEEKING AND KNOWING

THE WILL OF GOD. NONE CAN TRULY ENROLL IN THE SCHOOL OF OBEDIENCE UNTIL HE HAS DECIDED ONCE AND FOR ALL THAT HE WOULD DO THE WILL OF GOD THE MOMENT HE KNOWS IT. JESUS GREW IN SEEKING, KNOWING AND DOING GOD'S WILL.

In the rejection of His own will the Lord testified, *"My food is to do the will of him who sent me and to accomplish his work"* (John 4:34); *"Truly, truly I say to you, the Son can do nothing of his own accord, but only what he sees the Father doing; for whatever he does, that the Son does likewise. For the Father loves the Son, and shows him all that he himself is doing; and greater works than these will he show him, that you may marvel"* (John 5:19-20); *"I can do nothing on my own authority as I hear, I judge; and my judgment is just, because I seek not my own will but the will of him who sent me"* (John 5:30).

Even in Gethsemane the Lord Jesus prayed, *"Father, if thou art willing, remove this cup from me; nevertheless not my will, but thine be done.."*.(Luke 22:42). He did not know God's will in the matter yet He felt constrained to pray. He therefore, prayed but left it open. Because He did not know what God's will on the matter was, He began by praying, *"If thou art willing...,"* and ended with *"Nevertheless not my will but thine be done."* After He prayed that first time, He began to sense inwardly that the most likely thing was that the Father's will was that the cup should not pass from Him. He then prayed a second time, *"My Father, if this cannot pass unless I drink it, thy will be done"* (Matthew 26:42). Things were increasingly clear to Him but all was not finalized. He then went away and prayed the same thing, that is, *"My Father, if this cannot pass unless I drink it, thy will be done."* After that third time of praying, everything became clear to Him and He entered into full knowledge and full assurance that the Father's will was that He drank the cup. When He knew that, He stopped praying and moved into action. He told the disciples, *"Are you still sleeping and taking your rest? Behold the hour is at hand, and the Son of man is betrayed into the hands of sinners. Rise, let us be going; see, my betrayer is at hand"* (Matthew 26:45-46).

We can see that Jesus put aside His own will in everything and did the will of His Father. If He put aside His will then there is no one on Planet Earth who ought not to put aside his own will. This means that in everything I must put aside my own ways regardless of what potential I think they hold I must seek the will of the Lord in everything and once it is known, I must do it.

From the example of Jesus, there may be rare occasions in which a believer may be under so much pressure that even though he does not know the will of God, He feels obliged, pressed and squeezed so much that he has to pray before he has come to terms with the will of the Lord. In such circumstances, the believer must pray even as the Lord prayed saying to the Father, *"If Thou art willing...,"* and ending, *"Nevertheless not my will, but thine be done."* The believer could continue to pray that way while seeking God's will. When the will of God is clear, he must pray that it be done if he has discovered that the issue is the will of God or he must stop to pray about the issue immediately he discovers that it is not.

It should be realized that only on one occasion in His life did the Lord pray that way. In all the other situations, He either knew the will of God and therefore prayed it through at once or He prayed that the Father might reveal His will and kept asking the Father to show Him His will in the matter. He continued that way until the will of the Father was known and then He could pray that it be executed.

In the Gethsemane prayer, the Lord did something unusual which was perhaps owing to the pressure that was upon Him. Before He prayed He had confessed, *"My soul is very sorrowful even unto death; remain here and watch with me"* (Matthew 26:38). Usually He would have prayed seeking God's will. He would perhaps have prayed as follows, *"Father, is the cup Your will for me? Father, have You ordained that I drink the cup? Have You ordained that this cup should pass or should not pass over me?"* Normally He would have continued to pray and wait before the Father until He knew what the Father's will was. Then knowing that the Father's will was that He drink the cup, He would have prayed, *"Lord let the cup that You have ordained for Me to drink come to Me in Your timing and in the full measure that You ordained for Me. Lord, give Me grace to drink it in such a way that You receive full glory for it."*

PRAYING AHEAD OF TIME

Since the prayer under pressure may have an abnormal note, the best thing is for the believer to bring everything to God in prayer well ahead of time. The best thing is to seek God's will before the pressure of the circumstances surrounding the decision is upon him. Take for example, a young woman ought to sort out with the Lord in prayer what God's will concerning marriage for her is, before she receives a proposal. If she does that, she would seek, and know God's will clearly and calmly and then commit herself to do it. If she does not seek God's will well ahead of time but waits for an eligible young man to make a proposal that pleases her well, the best that she would be able to pray in honesty would be. *"Lord, let me marry this young man, nevertheless, not my will but thine be done."* Under such circumstances, she may not be able to pray in honesty because her will is already heavily inclined to the young man. The Lord Jesus was able to maintain a neutral position and seek God's will unbiased in a difficult situation. Because none of us has a will that is like His in everything, we should as much as possible avoid getting under the pressure from which He prayed as He prayed. If we do that we will be able to run a straight course.

Having written that, we must acknowledge that although most situations can be prayed through ahead of time emergencies will arise and compel us to pray that something happen the way we want if it is God's will. What we will be saying in those circumstances would be that we do not know God's will but we know our own will. We think that our will could be the same with God's. If that is the case, God should do His will which is at the same time our will. If on the other hand God sees that our will is different from His, He should leave ours aside and do His. Emergencies will come and may we pray with such vagueness. However, may such emergencies come only once or twice in very many years.

Jesus gave Himself so much to prayer. A good part of His prayer time must have been spent in seeking God's will and only a portion spent in pleading that that will be done. We have seen1 that the prayer life of Jesus was intensive and aggressive. That intensiveness and that aggression resulted from two factors: His labours to know God's will and His labours to ensure that the will of God that He knew passed into fulfilment. We too must aggressively seek God's will in prayer and once it is known we must intensively and aggressively pray until it is done. The Bible says, *"Upon your walls, O Jerusalem, I have set watchmen; all the day and all the night they shall never be silent. You who put the Lord in remembrance, take no rest, and give him no rest until he establishes Jerusalem and makes it a praise in the earth"* (Isaiah 62:6-7). Such wrestling night and day can only be carried out by those who know what God's will in a given situation is. May we be those ones and then we shall be fully blessed. Amen.

KNOWING GOD'S WILL

We have shown clearly the importance of praying according to the will of God. To be more exact, we have shown that because prayer is the bringing of God's will by His people to Him for execution, the knowledge of that will is a pre-requisite for prayer.

The question may arise as to how God's will can be known. We cannot treat the subject matter here since it will be treated in another book.2 Suffice it for the moment to say that the Lord has treated the subject most thoroughly in one verse - John 7:17 in which He says, *"If any man's will is to do his will, he shall know..."* The believer who uses his own will to commit himself totally and completely to the Lord Jesus; who uses his own will to will to do the will of the Lord will find that the Lord responds to him readily and reveals what His will is to him so that he may do it. God normally reveals His will readily to His obedient children for how He yearns that they would know and do it and so please His heart. All who want to do His will should truly will to do His will. Then they should ask Him to reveal His will to them and He will do it speedily. None can will to do God's will and seek truly to know that will and not know it.

THE FUNCTION OF THE HUMAN WILL

We have shown that a believer should put aside his own will and seek, know and do the will of the Lord. The question may then be asked as to whether the believer ought not to *"Throw away"* his will. We answer that he should. God created the believer's will for a specific purpose. The divine purpose for the believer's will is that it be used to will to do God's will. God will not will to do His will for the believer. The believer who does not actively use his will to do God's will will be seduced into passivity. God has ordained that the will be used to will to do God's will. The believer's will should be actively used to will do God's will. After the believer has used his will to will to know God's will, the must use his will to will to put his own will aside; use his will to will to seek God's will; use his will to will to know God's will and use his will to will to do God's will. If he does that he will be using his will in a God-ordained way and will thus escape the snare of the devil. Glory be to the Lord!

Those who are willing to know God's will but are not committed to doing it want to exercise their minds. God has no sympathy with such people and will actively hide his will from them. Only the obedient can continue to know God's will.

A personal question

I have proved over the last twenty-two years of walking with the Lord that continued revelation of God's will is conditioned on continued obedience. I have learnt that when obedience ends, revelation also ends. Since prayer that is useful is that which is a proclamation of God's will and since that will is always revealed to the obedient ones, is there any area of known disobedience to the will of God in your life? Before you answer, invite the Holy Spirit to search your heart and to reveal its hidden contents. If he shows you that there is no area of controversy between you and the Lord then you can and should go on and develop a more extensive and intensive prayer life. If he shows you that there is, then stop all else until you have put things right with Him. It is then that He will show you His will for today and enable you to do it. It is then that you will pray and be both blessed and heard. Praise the Lord!

7

· · · · · · · ·

Earth governed by heaven

We are trying to make it obvious that prayer should be according to the will of God for it to mean anything. We insist that a knowledge of God's will is all important. This need is made abundantly clear by the following study of Scripture.

Matthew 16:19 reads, *"I will give you the keys of the kingdom of heaven, and whatever you bind on earth shall be bound in heaven and whatever you loose on earth shall be loosed in heaven."*

Matthew 18:18 reads, *"Truly, I say to you, whatever you bind on earth shall be bound in heaven, and whatever you loose on earth shall be loosed in heaven."*

If these verses were really as they are quoted here, it would mean that Peter (16:19) and any disciple (18:18) had authority to impose his will on God the Father, God the Son, God the Holy Spirit and all the angels and other heavenly beings. This would make man *"God"* for he would just have to bind and heaven must bind or loose and heaven must loose. There would be no absolute need to seek God's will for God would be compelled to fit in with man.

However, these verses are not a very correct translation of the Greek. Many translators have pointed that out. In the notes at the bottom of the page where the first verse appears in the Hebrew-Greek Key Study Bible, the following has been written, *(A more accurate translation of this verse from the Greek3 is, *"And I will give thee the keys of the kingdom of the heavens. And whatever thou shall bind on the earth shall be as having been bound in the heavens; and whatever thou shall loose on the earth shall be as having been loosed in the heavens."* ...The teaching here is that those things which are conclusively decided by the King in the kingdom of heaven, having been so decided upon, are emulated by the Church on earth... We as believers can never make conducive decisions about things but can only confirm those decisions which have already been made by the king Himself as conclusive in the general context of His kingdom both on earth and in heaven. See Matthew 18:18 where the same two verbs, *"to bind"* and *"to loose,"* are said to be possessed by all disciples. The two verbs *"dedemenon"* and *"lelumenon"* are both perfect passive participles which should have been translated as *"having been bound"* and as *"having been loosed"* already in the heavens. Believers on earth can only confirm what has already taken place in heaven.)

We can now write the verse as it ought to read, *"I will give you the keys of the kingdom of heaven and whatever you bind on earth shall be, having been bound in heaven, and whatever you loose on earth shall be having been loosed in heaven."*

This means that if heaven has not bound, earth can bind for billions of years and nothing would be bound and if heaven has not loosed earth could loose everyday for billions of years and nothing would be actually loosed. If any individual binds on earth that which has not been bound in heaven, he is not only wasting time. He is resisting God for He wants His will to be done on earth as it is in heaven. He wants earth to be governed by heaven and not vice versa. The significance of this is that since what will ultimately prevail is the will of God and not the will of man; since what will be answered is only those prayers in which earth confirms that which has been already established in heaven, the one praying should exercise the wisdom of first finding out what has been bound and what has been loosed in heaven and then bind and loose accordingly. He will find out what God's will is and then pray that will into existence. This is wisdom. Praise the Lord.

8
* * * * * * * *

God's will in man's personal needs

We have continued to insist that the knowledge of God's will is fundamental to all true praying. We have insisted that the first part of prayer should be the seeking of God's will and when that will is known, it should then be prayed through.

Having said that, some one may ask, *"Do I not have the freedom to ask God to supply my daily needs? Do I not have the freedom to ask the Lord to give me the desires of my heart?"*

Our reply is that the believer has much liberty. The Lord has encouraged all who are His to ask and they would receive. For example He says, *"Hitherto you have asked nothing in my name; ask and you will receive, that your joy may be full"* (John 16:24).

The question remains as to whether the believer always knows what his real needs are! How many of God's children know themselves enough to ask those things which when given would cause their joy to be full? My experience with myself and from counselling many believers is that we do not know what we need. This may seem to be startling but let me explain.

First of all, the Lord has committed Himself to supply our needs and not our wants. The exhortation of the apostle is *"My God will supply every need of yours according to his riches in glory in Christ Jesus"* (Philippians 4:19). Many of us present our wants to God and not our needs. We ask but do not receive because we ask wrongly to spend what we receive from asking on our passions. We must agree with the Lord that our hearts are what He says they are. The prophet confessed, *"The heart is deceitful above all things and desperately corrupt; who can understand it?"* (Jeremiah 17:9). I must confess that in the early years of my walk with God I did not come to terms with the fact that my heart was desperately corrupt and deceitful. Now I am more aware of the corruption and the deceitfulness of my heart not because my heart has become more corrupt and more deceitful (I hope not!) but because I have received more light than I received in the past. I want to confess that I am beginning to be truly afraid of what I think I know, knowing how deceitful I could be. I am beginning to be afraid of what I think I have seen, knowing how false or how confused and how dim my sight may be. These things have made me not to be too sure, on my own, as to what my needs are. They have made me see the necessity of praying often to the Father as follows: *"My Lord and my God. I acknowledge the deep corruption and deceitfulness of my heart. I realise as never before the fact that I often confuse my wants with my needs. I confess the fact that often what I thought I needed one day has become different afterwards. Lord, I refuse to count on myself. I need You to show me what my true needs are. Lord, what is my true need in this area and that area and the other area? Lord, I confess that do not know. However, Lord, let me present my thoughts to You so that You may know me. In this area I think my need is…. In that area I think my need is…and in that other area I think my need is…. Lord, ignore what I think. I am waiting on You. Lord reveal to me what my true need is. I refuse to ask*

You to give me what I want. I am waiting for You to reveal to me what You know to be my need. When You do that then I would ask You to supply them. Lord, deliver me from the impatience of attempting to supply my own needs by myself. Lord deliver me from the deception of confusing the voice of my own spirit for Your voice. My Father, speak so that Your servant may make progress. Lord, do it. Lord do it."

I confess that God has often answered me and made me know what my needs were. Sometimes He has shown me that my needs were what I initially presented to Him. At other times He has shown me that my needs were very different from what I thought. At other times He has rebuked me for ever having certain desires. It has been a school. It is an on-going school. The Holy Spirit has been the Teacher in this school of revealing God's will to me. I confess that I am the happy student. I confess that from the time that I began to ask the Lord to show me what my needs were and began to actively refrain from aggressive and intensive prayer about anything until I have known the will of God, things have changed a great deal. I am still learning and the Holy Spirit is patiently teaching; A blessed future is ahead. Praise the Lord.

The fact that God has commanded us to ask and we shall receive does not absolve us from the responsibility to knowing the will of God and consequently asking according to His will for us. Let me illustrate this with an example from Scripture. The Bible says, *"Now when Elisha had fallen side with the illness of which he was to die, Joash king of Israel went down to him, and wept before him, crying, My father, my father! The chariots of Israel and its horsemen!"* And Elisha said to him, *"Take a bow and arrows"*; so he took a bow and arrows. Then he said to the king of Israel, *"Draw the bow"*; and he drew it. And Elisha laid his hands upon the king's hands. And he said, *"Open the window eastward"*; and he opened it. Then Elisha said, *"Shoot"*; and he shot. And he said, *"The Lord's victory over Syria! For you shall fight the Syrians in Aphek until you have made an end of them."* And he said, *"Take the arrows"*; and he took them. And he said to the king of Israel, *"Strike the ground with them"*; and he struck three times, and stopped. Then the man of God was angry with him, and said, *"You should have struck five or six times; then you would have struck down Syria until you had made an end of it, but now you will strike down Syria only three times"* (2 Kings 13:14-19).

We see here that the king set limitations to how many times he would have struck Syria because he did not ask how many times he was to strike. He thought he knew and the prophet allowed the king's thoughts to be established even though they fell short of the desired end. Had he been humble enough to have asked the prophet, *"How many arrows shall I take?"* He would have been told to take five or six. Later on, he would have asked, *"How many times should I strike the ground with the arrows?"* He would have been h*told; *"five or six times."* He would have stricken the ground five or six times and that would have led him to strike down Syria until an end was made of it. We see clearly that an enemy only received partial crushing because a king took upon himself the responsibility of deciding how many arrows he was to take and how many times he was to strike the ground. I wonder how many victories we have known only in part or not known at all because we took the decision to ask God according to what we felt or wanted instead of according to what He showed us! We may think that we are exercising our freedom but O, what exercise of freedom! O that we would exercise our freedom of asking God what our real needs are and then to pray them through after He has shown us. Then we shall be truly blessed! Then we shall not limit or frustrate the designs or desires of God's heart.

Let us take another example from human life; Many young men between twenty and thirty go to the Lord with lists of characteristics that they want in the wife they want. The list is drawn on the basis of their present knowledge of themselves and their circumstances. They are sincere but they may be sincerely mistaken. They see their circumstances only in part. They do not know the future. God on the other hand knows their circumstances in full and knows all of the future. They ought to pray and say, *"Lord, You know my circumstance and the future in full. You know what I am and what I am going to be. You know what this town, nation, continent and planet is going to be in the years ahead. You know the details of all the girls now and in the future. Lord, show me the characteristics that best fit the woman who will best help me to accomplish Your call on my life. Lord, show me those characteristics so that I may ask for them of You in prayer. Lord, show me those characteristics and help me in my development to become the man that would be satisfied with them. Lord, do it."*

If someone handled the matter that way, he would truly be led of the Lord!

There are many things that may alter in the future which a young man of twenty to thirty may not know and which would affect his marriage life. For example, he may be leading a quiet life now whereas God has ordained that he will move into a ministry in the future that would take him away from home very often. If he is thinking that his life will be simple and quiet in the future, he may be looking for a quiet woman who would lean heavily on an always available husband. He would consequently ignorantly ask God for such a wife. They may be happy until his circumstances change and he moves on with

God into that area of ministry that would take him away from home very often. He would then find that the wife who would have been most suitable would have been a more independent woman with a clear sense of leadership and initiative who would be able to take care of their children and home and provide leadership in his absence. If he had asked the Lord, the Lord would have shown him that he should ask Him for a woman who has leadership capabilities, a clear sense of initiative and who is able to love and live happily with a man who would be gone most of the time. These characteristics might at first disturb him but as he yielded to God and received them in the wife he would marry, he would also pray to become the man to fit with such a wife. Years later on, as his ministry develops he would see clearly why God ordained that type of a wife for him and be grateful as things fit into focus. Truly we do not know what we need. We must ask God to reveal our needs to us so that we can ask and receive them from Him in prayer.

I am writing this chapter in a hotel room in the city of Bombay in India. My wife and our children have been involved in a long fast of forty days just before I left home. This means that we did not have much time as a family since. I was also) on the writing of the preceding book. I will be away for forty days and one week after my return home, I will start my own forty day fast for the overthrow of the *"prince of Islam."* This means that we do not have much time together as a regular family. The reality is that neither my wife nor myself knew that such a life was waiting for us when we first met as teenagers and got engaged to each other. Even ten years ago we could not have guessed that our ministry would take us beyond our country and continent but by the will of God it has. My beloved wife has adjusted successfully to our type of life and I thank the

Lord very much for it. However, if I knew what I now know I would have prayed for her differently during our courtship and the first years of our marriage. That would have opened more room for the Lord to prepare her for her present role. Yes, God has worked mightily in her but how mightier would have been His work had I asked and received from the Lord the characteristics that she needed and prayed for their rapid formation in her from the age of eighteen when we first met. She would have enjoyed twenty-five years of special dealing with God in answer to prayer all these years.

I am not saying that God is necessarily limited by our ignorance. He could act independently of our knowledge and our co-operation through praying. However, that is not His normal way of working. Even when He does move in that direction, we are the losers for we were created to co-operate with Him by praying His will back to Him for execution. We lose much when He has to act without our prayers and sometimes, nothing would cause Him to act if we do not pray.

The matter of seeking God's will in personal matters must not just be limited to major issues. It must be brought down to all the affairs of life. Take for example that a brother feels that he should go and visit another brother in the next city. Without seeking the Lord's will, he sets out to ask the Lord for transportation, journeying mercies and the like. He then goes to visit this brother only to discover that he has moved out of town because of an urgent matter which he did not foresee. The one who goes to visit him has thus spent his money, time and effort in vain. Had he asked the Lord, he would have been shown that he should not go. The reason might not have been given to him (for God does not delight in giving reasons before events occur) but he would have been told not to go and in obedience he would have stayed back and saved himself the loss of time, money and all.

I am quite encouraged by the way that David sought the Lord about His will in his personal matters that I will quote two examples here from Scripture: *"Now they told David, Behold, the Philistines are fighting against Keilah, and are robbing the threshing floors."* There David inquired of the Lord, *"Shall I go and attack these Philistines?"* And the Lord said to David, *"Go and attack the Philistines and save Keilah. But David's men said to him,"* Behold, we are afraid here in Judah; how much more then if we go to Keilah against the armies of the Philistines? *"Then David inquired of the Lord again. And the Lord answered him,"* Arise, go down to Keilah; for I will give the Philistines into your hand. *"And David and his men went to Keilah, and fought with the Philistines, and brought away their cattle, and made a great slaughter among them. So David delivered the inhabitants of Keilah"* (1 Samuel 23:1-5). David had the thought in his mind. He did not act upon it. Rather he sought God's will about the matter. As he sought the Lord, he was shown what God's will in the matter was. He then turned to his people who were of a contrary opinion. He did not say, *"Well, since my people do not see with me, I will abandon the matter."* He had his desire. God showed him that his desire was His. His people did not see with him. He, therefore, brought the issue up again with the Lord. The Lord encouraged him to move ahead. He moved ahead and saw the victory of the Lord. It was a risky situation but he derived courage from the fact that God had promised him victory. May we too learn how to bring our thoughts and desires before the Lord and seek His will. May we learn how to go back to God and seek His will in the face of opposition. May we then come to full assurance about the will of God in an issue and may we then relentlessly pray it through and we shall be blessed indeed.

In another incident the Bible says, *"When Abiatha the son of Ahimelech fled to David to Keilah, he came down with an ephod in his hand. Now it was told Saul that David had come to Keilah. And Saul said, God has given him into my hand; for he has shut himself in by entering a town that has gates and bars. And Saul summoned all the people to war, to go down to Keilah, to besiege David and his men. David knew that Saul was plotting evil against him; and he said to Abiathar the priest, Bring the ephod here. Then said David, O Lord, the God of Israel, thy servant has surely heard that Saul seeks to come to Keilah, to destroy the city on my account. Will the men of Keilah surrender me into his hand? Will Saul come down, as thy servant has heard? O Lord, the God of Israel, I beseech thee, tell, thy servant. And the Lord said, He will surely come down. Then said David, Will the men of Keilah surrender me and my men into the hand of Saul? And the Lord said, They will surrender you. Then David and his men, who were about six hundred, arose and departed from Keilah, and they went wherever they could go. When Saul was told that David had escaped from Keilah, he gave up the expedition"* (1 Samuel 23:6-13).

Had David operated on the natural plane, he would have said, *"I saved these people. They will surely protect me and not give me to Saul,"* If he had thought that way, he would have relaxed and not escaped. Saul would have gone there and perhaps that would have the end of his life, his team and above all, it would have been the end of the kingdom!

May we too learn to take nothing for granted but take the responsibility to seek to know and to do God's will in all the details of our lives. Praise the Lord!

9
• • • • • • • •

The dangers of the permissive will of God

No one should think that he has freedom to come before the God of heaven and ask anything that he wants and then leave it to God to sort out if the thing is according to His will is just cast away by the Lord and all that the person who prayed such a prayer suffers is the fact that he wasted time. Prayer is a more serious issue than that. Human words do not go a God and produce no effect or consequence.

When a person prays according to the will of God, the Lord rejoices and answers to the blessing of the person who prayed. The Bible says, *"And this is the confidence that we have in him, that if we ask anything according to his will he hears us. And if we know that he hears us in whatever we ask, we know that we have obtained the requests made of him"* (1 John 5:14-15). Believers ought to always labour to pray according to God's will.

When a person prays ignorantly outside God's will, the Lord forgives him and no harm may come to him, for his prayer. However, the person who prays ignorantly outside God's will where the ignorance is the fruit of laziness in seeking God's will with the whole heart, there is some harm that the person suffers for failure to know God's will because of laziness.

When a person knows that a certain thing is not God's will but decides to desire it and to ask for it in prayer, the Lord will let him have what he has asked for to his immediate or long term undoing. We can illustrate intentionally praying outside God's will as follows:

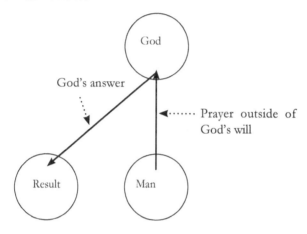

What happens to prayer that is outside the will of God.

Let us look at two examples of such prayers from the Word of God.

The rabble in the wilderness

The Bible says, *"A mixed multitude also went up with them, and very many cattle, and both flocks and herds"* (Exodus 12:38). *"Now the rabble (mixed multitude) that was among them had a strong craving; and the people of Israel also wept again, and said, O that we had meat to eat! We remember the fish we ate in Egypt for nothing, the cucumbers, the melons, the leeks, the onions and the garlic; but now our strength is dried up, and there is nothing at all but this manna to look at."* (Numbers 11:4-6). *"Moses heard the people weeping throughout their families, every man at the door of his tent, and the anger of the Lord blazed hotly, and Moses was displeased"* (Numbers 11:10). *"And the Lord said to Moses, Say to the people, Consecrate yourselves for tomorrow, and you shall eat meat; for you have wept in the hearing of the Lord, saying, Who will give us meat to eat? For it was well with us in Egypt. Therefore the Lord will give you meat, and you shall eat. You shall not eat one day, or two days, or five days, or ten days, or twenty days, but a whole month, until it comes out of your nostrils and becomes loathsome to you, because you have rejected the Lord who is amongst you, and have wept before him, saying, Why did we come forth out of Egypt?"* (Numbers 11:18-20).

"And there went forth a wind from the Lord, and it brought quails from the sea, and let them fall besides the camp, about a day's journey on this side and a day's journey on the other side, round about the camp, and about two cubits above the face of the earth. And the people rose all that day, and all night, and all the next day, and gathered the quails; he who gathered least gathered ten homers; and thy spread them out for themselves all around the camp. While the meat was yet between their teeth, before it was consumed, the anger of the Lord was kindled against the people, and the Lord smote the people with a very great plague. Therefore the name of that place was called Kibrothhattaavah because there they buried the people who had the craving" (Numbers 11:31-34).

"They had a wanton craving in the wilderness, and put God to the test in the desert; he gave them what they asked, but sent a wasting disease among them" (Psalm 106:14-15).

They desired meat even though they did not need it. They cried for meat and despised the manna which the Lord had provided for them and which satisfied their need but not their lust. They moved on the plane of lust, of covetousness, of desires that were rooted in self and not in need or in the Lord.

The Lord was offended, gave them what they asked for plus a deadly bonus - the plague.

There are many today who are like the rabble in the wilderness. They are in the Church but their hearts have not been circumcised from a love of the world and a love for the things of the world. They crave after one worldly thing or the other and after one worldly position and then another. The Lord looks at such hearts and sometimes gives them what they desire plus leanness of soul. At other times he is offended and gives them leanness of soul without even letting them have what they desire.

Each person must examine the desires of his heart and see if they are also the desires of the heart of God. When a person finds that there are desires in his heart that do not correspond to the desires on God's heart, he should repent of them immediately and be cleansed of them. It is not enough to say that they are only desires and not prayers. There is a sense in which the desires of the hearts of men flow to God as prayer even without the person consciously asking. There is a sense in which all desires are prayers for all that is on the heart is before God. He sees it and acts accordingly. Purity of desire and conformity of desire to the will of God is indispensable to spiritual health. May God's children take note. May they settle it once and for ever that they will not permit anything which they know for certain not to be the will of God to last another second in their hearts. May they be merciful and correct other members of the body who are asking in dangerous ignorance! Praise the Lord!

10

•••••••

The will of God that is already known

We have stressed the importance of seeking and knowing the will of God before requests are made to Him. We have established that it is dangerous to present man's thoughts and ways to God, insisting that He approves these instead of seeking and knowing His thoughts and His ways and presenting those to Him.

In order to make one thing clearer, we want to say something about the will of God that is already known and about which it would be sin to seek it any further or to ask Him in prayer. There are many aspects of the Christian life in which the will of the Lord is plain. There are other areas in which His will has been plainly revealed in Scripture. For such areas, the praying believer knows the thoughts and the ways of God and should immediately get into prayer of refrain from praying. Let us look at some examples.

No one should pray seeking God's will as to whether he should commit sin or not. The will of God is clear and has been stated clearly in the Word that none should sin. God will not permit anyone to commit sin. To seek His will about committing sin is the same as asking Him to let you do what He does not want. Such asking is rebellion and He may well allow the rebel to have what he wants.

No one should ask the Lord, *"Lord, should I pray about the salvation of this person? Is it Your will that he be saved?"* Here again the will of God is clear and it has already been revealed to all men. The Bible says, *"The Lord is not slow about his promise as some count slowness, but is forbearing toward you, not wishing that any should perish, but that all should reach repentance"* (2 Peter 3:9). A believer should be able to pray for the salvation of thousands of people without asking God what His will is.

However, in the praying for the salvation of an individual there may be cause to seek revelation in order to better pray. Take for example that one is praying for the salvation of Mr. X. It may be necessary to ask the Lord to reveal what is holding him captive. It could be women; it could be drugs; it could be the fear of being persecuted or it could be that the family has been held captive by a certain medium for years and consequently he is bound. If after praying for his salvation for some time there seems to be no response. The praying person needs to ask the Lord, *"Father, show me what is keeping him away from coming to You."* The Lord will graciously reveal where the problem is. Once the problem is known, more accurate praying can then follow. For example, for a man who is held captive by a medium, the praying person would intercede that the Lord might set him free from captivity to that medium so that he might be able to come to the Lord. A man who is held captive by an immoral relationship might be prayed for by asking the Lord to open his eyes to the futility of such a relationship or the Lord might be importuned to make the relationship distasteful or the woman holding the man captive might be commanded, *"In the name of Jesus I command you to get out of this man's life, from now and never to come back into his life."* Such commanding which follows revelation often leads to the captive being set free to turn to the Lord Jesus. So even in cases where the general will of God is known, the Lord still needs to be sought for details that will enable one to pray effectively.

Someone may ask, *"Do I need to have such details about what is keeping the person away in order to pray for his salvation?"* The answer is that for general praying, such details are not necessary. However for specific praying, they are indispensable.

YOUR MIND MATTERS

We have stressed the importance of receiving revelation from the Lord in order to pray according to His will. This should not be understood as a call to put away our minds. The Lord did not make man and the devil gave him a brain. God made man and gave him a mind. The praying believer should use his mind. However the mature believer understands that not all that comes into his mind is from the Lord. Some of his thoughts come from the world or the flesh. Some may even be injected by the wicked one. Others may come from his own spirit whereas others come from the Holy Spirit through his spirit. By learning to discern the source of the information that comes into his mind, he will learn to reject what should be rejected and we what should be used. We only say that he must use his mind as well as his spirit. He must prayerfully bring up to the Lord what he has received in his spirit and as he prays, seeking light from the Lord, he will be helped to come to a knowledge of what the will of God is and so pray according to that will.

THINGS IN WHICH GOD'S WILL IS NOT OBVIOUS

We have said that there is no reason in seeking God's will in matters in which the will of the Lord is obvious. However, when it comes to fine details, there are many things about which the will of God still needs to be sought even though the overall direction of God's will is known. Let us come back to the matter of reaching someone with the gospel. It is perfectly correct that prayer be offered to the Lord for the person's salvation. However, the person praying for the man's salvation may also begin to pray about how the person will be reached with the gospel. He could just pray that the person be reached with the gospel. He may on the other hand ask the Lord to show him to what method of evangelism the person is most likely to yield. Some people are open to direct contact by personal communication, others respond more to literature evangelism and others are best reached by radio. The person who is praying for the person being reached with the gospel and who in addition asks and receives from the Lord the method of evangelism to which the person would be most opened will pray that the Lord would lead the person to being reached that way.

SPECIFICITY LEADS TO BETTER PRAYING

It is a must that the believer prays. However the quantity and quality of prayer matters. We should pray more quantitative and more qualitative prayers. We should pray more prayers of the right kind. A child can pray, *"Lord save the lost in Africa"* and it will be alright. An adult can also pray that way if there is no other way by which he may receive more information!

However, there is a world of difference between that kind of prayer and the praying for a Mr. X who lives in town Y and has heard the gospel from childhood and knows intellectually that Jesus is the Son of God and the Way back to the Lord but is afraid that if he gives his life to the Lord, his chances of being promoted by his godless boss would be greatly reduced. Such details would enable a man to pray abundantly. They will lead to wrestling with God and wrestling against the Enemy. All who want to make progress in praying must do all they can to receive all the light that they can receive on the issue being prayer about. The light that can be received from man should be received and the light that can be received only from the Lord should be received. With all the light that can be received available, the praying person can fully do the most important business on earth - pray quantitatively and qualitatively and God will answer. Praise the Lord!

11

....

Spiritual maturity and knowing the will of God

The way in which we have approached the matter of receiving the will of God and praying it through is that which will characterize young believers most of the time and mature believers only occasionally.

The difference lies in the fact that young believers are full of their own thoughts and ideas. They have long lists of things that they want God to give them and to do for them. They are not schooled in walking quietly with God. The result of this is that the will of God for them will come often through their asking questions like the following. 1. Lord, I want this thing. Is it Your will that I have it? 2. Lord, I want You to do this for me. Does the desire originate from me or it is You who has put it into me? 3. Lord, I want this spiritual gift. Have you ordained me to have it. 4. Lord, I want to become a great evangelist. Show me if that is what You want me to become. 5. Lord, I want to go here and do this kind of thing for Your glory. Lord show me if that is what You want, and so on. The ideas start in him and he is sorting them out - for their origin and divine confirmation. There is little that he receives directly from God.

We must say that this kind of attitude is not bad. In fact, it has its place in the Christian life and it should be used. However, as a person matures in the knowledge and love of the Lord, his pre-occupation would be communion with God. He would increasingly come before the Lord to worship and to praise Him. He would come to Him at other times to give an account of what happened during his discharge of the last commands that the Lord gave him. So, his pre-occupation will be being in the Lord's presence. As he spends time in God's presence, he will not be pre-occupied with seeking God's will about numerous things that he wants to do but will rather just wait for orders.

As he waits before the Lord in silence, the Lord will then give him instructions, *"Go and do this and that for Me. Go and do it this way and at this time and when you would have finished, come back and let me know."* The believer has thus received the will of God and can go straight away into praying it back to the Lord. He may then move into prayer saying, *"Lord, grant that I will be able to do this thing that You have sent me to do. Lord give me the strength, anointing and wisdom that I need to do this thing that You have asked me to do. Lord, grant that this project that You have entrusted into my hands will succeed."*

We see this happening a lot in the life of Moses:

    a. And God said to Moses (Exodus 6:2)

    b. And the Lord said to Moses (Exodus 6:10

    c. The Lord said to Moses (Exodus 6:29)

    d. And the Lord said to Moses (Exodus 7:1)

    e. And the Lord said to Moses and Aaron (Exodus 7:8)

    f. Then the Lord said to Moses (Exodus 7:14)

    g. And the Lord said to Moses (Exodus 7:19

h. Then the Lord said to Moses (Exodus 8:1)

i. And the Lord said to Moses (Exodus 8:5)

j. Then the Lord said to Moses (Exodus 8:16)

k. Then the Lord said to Moses (Exodus 8:20)

The same thing was clearly manifested in the life of Elijah. Again let us look at a few examples in his life:

a. And the word of the Lord came to him (1 Kings 17:2)

b. Then the word of the Lord came to him (1 Kings 17:8)

c. After many days the word of the Lord came to Elijah (1 Kings 18:1)

The same thing was evident in the apostle Paul's life:

a. *"...and saw him saying to me"* (Acts 22:18)

b. *"And he said to me"* (Acts 22:21)

c. *"The following night the Lord stood by him and said"* (Acts 18:11)

Of course these people did initiate things some times by being the first to talk to God but often the Lord took the initiative.

We can illustrate these two positions as follows:

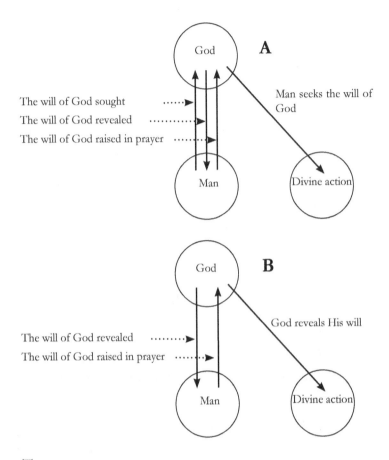

TWO POSITIONS IN PRAYER

(A) Man seeks God's

(B) God reveals His will.

The important thing to bear in mind is that the really crucial issue is that God's will is done and that the believer co-operate through prayer for this to come to pass. All believers will experience (A) and (B). Less mature and consequently less spiritual believers will live more in the realm of (A) and only occasionally experience (B). Those who know their God and live in His presence increasingly will experience more of (B) and less of (A).

KNOWING GOD'S WILL SPONTANEOUSLY

The believer will start by asking God's will in each situation. As he grows up, he will grow in the knowledge of God's will so much that when he faces a situation, he would intuitively know what the will of God is without going through the process of asking it is His will. He will then be able to respond and pray according to the will of God spontaneously. This is the pathway along which we should all walk. The apostle Paul exhorts, *"Therefore do not be foolish but understand what the will of the Lord is"* (Ephesians 5:17). The only problem is that some believers who are not spiritual would presume that they are spiritual and in the face of a situation be led by their minds or spirits instead of the Holy Spirit. They would presume that they know the will of God and then begin to pray on the basis of a false assumption. The safe guard is for believers to consider themselves as immature or able to be mistaken and consequently ask and know God's will before beginning to wrestle it through.

Those who are truly mature know themselves. They have known the Cross's dealing with the self-life for many years and also known the Holy Spirit for many years that they can know from the word *"go"* if something has its origin in their spirits or in the Holy Spirit. Through numerous experiences of unmistaken leading, they come to be trustworthy and yet they walk along that path with deep humility for they know that none is ever too mature to be mistaken. Praise the Lord!

12
....

The desires of the heart

We have sought to make it abundantly clear that God's will should be sought, known and then prayed through. We have sought to show that this should be done in everything.

The question may arise in some hearts as to what should be done with the desires of the heart and with those Scriptures that promise that they will be granted.

It is true that the word of God promises that the desires of the heart will be granted. Below are some of those Scriptures:

1. *"In thy strength the king rejoices, O Lord; and in thy help how greatly he exults! Thou hast given him his heart's desire, and has not withheld the request of his lips"* (Psalm 21:1-2)

2. *"The Lord answer you in the day of trouble! The name of the God Jacob protect you! May he remember all your offerings and regard with favour your burnt sacrifices! May he grant you your heart's desire, and fulfil all your plans! May we shout for joy over your victory, and in the name of our God set up our banners! May the Lord fulfil all your petitions!"* (Psalm 20:1-5).

3. *"He fulfils the desire of all who fear him, he also hears their cry, and saves them. The Lord preserves all who love him; but all the wicked he will destroy"* (Psalm 146:19-20).

4. *"Take delight in the Lord, and he will give you the desires of your heart. Commit your way to the Lord; trust in him, and he will act"* (Psalm 37:4-5).

5. *"Ask, and it will be given you; seek, and you will find; knock, and it will be opened to you. For every one who asks receives, and he who seeks finds, and to him who knocks it will be opened. Or what man of you, if his son asks him for bread, will give him a stone? Or if he asks for a fish, will give him a serpent? If you then, who are evil, know how to give good gifts to your children, how much more will your Father who is in heaven give good things to those who ask him!"* (Matthew 7:7-11).

It is indeed true that children may come to the Lord and ask Him to give them the desires of their hearts. God will decide what is good for the child and give him. He will refuse to give those desires that are not good for the child. In this case the child does not know what is good or not good for him and therefore, leaves God to choose what he should have. We encourage children to pray that way. They should bring and present the desires of their hearts to God. He will sort them out and answer them accordingly.

However, what can be tolerated and even accepted from a child cannot be expected to come from an adult. The adult knows his father. He who knows what things the father is likely to give him if he asks and what things are most unlikely to be given. Where he does not know he would ask the father before the request is formulated and presented to the father.

In the passages quoted above, we read in one of them that, *"May he grant you your heart's desires."* This could mean that God gives what the heart is to desire or that He gives the things that the heart desires. I think it is both. God first gives the believer what to desire. In this way the desires of the believer have their origin in the Lord. They are His will. After He has given him what to desire, and the believer has learnt to desire what God gave him to desire, God then goes ahead and grants the things desired. We can illustrate this way:

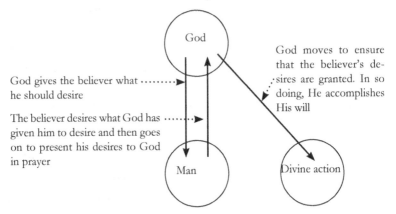

God grants the desires of the heart

The other thing to be taken into consideration is that the believer is exhorted to take delight in the Lord and then the Lord will give him the desires of his heart (Psalm 37:4). The believer who takes delight in the Lord will seek to know what God desires. He will then make the desires of God his desires. He will also seek to know what God delights in and he will labour to ensure that he delights in what God delights in. In this way, the desires of his heart will be the will of God which he has sought, known and made his delight. So, as the Lord moves to give him the desires of his heart, He is actually moving to accomplish His will. This is actually what God wants. He wants His children to seek His will, know it, delight in it and then make it their delight; then present their delight to Him to execute. We can illustrate it as follows:

1. The believer delights in the Lord.
2. The believer in his delight seeks God's will.
3. The believer then knows God's will delightedly.
4. The believer learns to delight in God's will.
5. By delighting in God's will the believer puts aside his own will and makes God's will in which he delights his own will.
6. The believer then delightedly presents his will to the Lord.
7. The Lord joyfully grants the desires of the believer's heart thereby also fulfilling the desires of His own.

Is it not a wonderful thing if we grow into the maturity that gives God the twin pleasure of satisfying our hearts and His in one act? Let us press on to that.

BETWEEN REVELATION AND ASKING

It is becoming evident that asking may not immediately following revelation. It could mean that there is a time lapse between the time that the believer receives the revelation and the time he prays it through. We shall look at that in a separate chapter.

13
•••••••

Receiving the will of God and spiritual enlargement

There is a sense in which no human being can receive all of the will of God about any matter. This is because it requires equality of the Spirit of impartation and the spirit of receptivity. The Holy Spirit is the one who imparts the will of God. He, the Holy Spirit receives all the will of God. He desires to impart all of it to man. Even when the spirit of man is pure and normal, He can only impart that which man can receive. This means that the quantity of the will of God that a man does receive is proportional to the size of his heart. This means that a young believer with a pure and normal spirit will not receive what a mature believer with a pure and normal spirit can receive.

In other words, the Holy Spirit will impart to a man what his spirit can receive and contain and not just what is in Him. This brings us to the matter of an enlarged spirit.

The Psalmist confessed, *"I will run in the way of thy commandments when thou enlargest my understanding"* (Psalm 119:32). The Lord can enlarge the spirit, soul and body. We see this quite readily in the physical realm when a short leg is caused to grow instantly and a so on. It also happens in the realm of the soul. In fact it should even happen more in the realm of the spirit since God works from the spirit outwards.

God does the enlargement of the spirit either immediately or as a gradual process. The believer whose eyes are open should pray that the Lord would enlarge his spirit so that he can receive more of the will of God. He should ask and keep asking. He should ask and keep pleading. He should refuse to accept a *"no"* from the Lord. As he asks he should expect God to carry out instant and progressive enlargement of the heart. He will know when he has received a sudden enlargement of heart and he should thank God for it. He will find out after some time that his heart has been enlarged. This was owing to the work of enlargement of the heart as a process. The one who has received an enlarged heart by whatever method God chose to enlarge it should continue to ask for further enlargement. He should at the same time actively strengthen his heart to carry more revelation from God and pray it through. Deep calls for deep. The large calls for enlargement. May the mature see this.

Understandably, there is a process of enlargement of heart that goes on in consecrated believers as they walk with the Lord even if they do not ask for it and pray for it. This is unconscious progressive enlargement. God sometimes also carries out sudden enlargement of some hearts without being asked to do so. However the best is reserved for those who in addition to receiving what comes to them as God's gift without their asking, go ahead and receive that which He gives as an addition to those who ask.

If you mean business about making progress in the prayer life, decide among other things that you will ask and receive an enlarged heart from the Lord and that you will continue to ask and receive until God finds in you a heart that can contain large portions of His will. You will then find that as you pray, you are able to cause some of the great and far-reaching desires and designs of God to come to pass. Praise the Lord.

14

• • • • • • • •

Receiving the will of God and spiritual sensitivity

We have just mentioned the need of an enlarged heart so that as much as possible of the will of God is received, mountained and prayed through. There is another side to the matter. Receiving all of the will of God is not only a matter of the dimensions of the heart. It is also a matter of how sensitive the heart it. The sensitive heart will receive the *"fine details"* from the Lord whereas the enlarged heart will receive the gross structure.

Solomon asked the Lord, *"Give thy servant therefore an understanding mind to govern thy people, that I may discern between good and evil"* (1 Kings 3:9). The soul can be given the capacity to discern. The spirit also can be given the capacity to discern and the body also can discern. If Solomon asked and received the capacity to discern with the mind, the consecrated believer can also ask and receive from the Father the capacity to discern in his spirit.

So, the will of God should be received quantitatively and qualitatively. The one who has asked and received an enlarged heart from the Lord should also ask that the Lord may give his enlarged heart spiritual sensitivity so that he will discern the fine details of the will of God.

This is all important because the Lord is not only committed to His will in general. He is committed to His will in detail. He wants things done by specific individuals at specific places for specific purposes, for specific durations. To miss any of these is to pray a bit off the target.

When the Lord wanted the tabernacle built, He took Moses aside and showed him how it was to be built. He went into specific details. Let us just look at the instructions of one of the items that had to be built. The Bible says, *"And you shall make a table of acacia wood; two cubits shall be its length, a cubit its breath, and a cubit and a half its height. You shall overlay it with pure gold, and make a molding of gold around it. And you shall make around it a frame a handbreadth wide, and a molding of gold around the frame. And you shall make for it four rings of gold, and fasten the rings to the four corners at its four legs. Close to the frame the rings shall lie, as holders for the poles to carry the table. You shall make the poles of acacia wood, and overlay them with gold, and the table shall be carried with these. And you shall make its plates and dishes for incense, and its flagons and bowls with which to pour libations; of pure gold you shall make them. And you shall set the bread of the Presence on the table before me always"* (Exodus 25:23-30).

It can be seen here that God is clearly committed to fine structure. This means that if a person does not develop the spiritual capacities to receive and to discern spiritual fine structure, there may be areas in which he will not be able to pray aright. In the example which we have just cited from the book of Exodus, the person who just prayed, *"Lord, grant that there be a table built for Your tabernacle"*, would be praying like a child. If God were to answer that prayer, what type of table should He produce? The prayer says nothing about the type of wood to be used in the construction of the table. It says nothing about the dimensions and leaves out what the table is to be overlaid with as well as all other details. A person could pray *"Lord, grant that there be a table built for Your tabernacle,"* every day for years and not be heard by the Lord. Because he has not given the details to the Lord, the Lord is not *"able"* to produce the desired table.

It is important in prayer that a person should pray as if God knows nothing about the matter he is pleading about. He should pray as if everything depends on what he tells the Lord. He should pray knowing that God will give him what he has asked. He should not expect God to include what he has refused to include in his asking.

We know that the Lord will do exceedingly abundantly more than we ask or think. This is not an invitation to laziness or to ignorance. If the Lord multiplies what I give by three then the person who asks for three things will receive nine things which the person who asks for ten thousand will receive thirty thousands. The same thing applies to quality. The Lord will add details to what we ask but the details will always be proportional to what we ask from the beginning.

As we have seen, prayer is seeking, knowing and praying the will of God back to Him. To limit Him by receiving His will without the details that He has included is to limit Him severely.

Those who want to make the most progress in prayer must grow in spiritual sensitivity. Lord, lead us that way. Amen.

15

....

Receiving the will of God and a spiritual walk

We have just written about the necessity for the praying believer to have an enlarged and an enlarging heart and to have a sensitive heart that is continuing to grow in spiritual sensitivity.

We have shown that the enlargement heart and the sensitivity of the heart can be asked and received from the Lord. On the other hand we want it to be understood that these cannot be asked and received independently of what a man's spiritual walk is. There are something that regardless of how fervently a baby asks they will not be given to him. If God gave us just everything we asked for, we would long since possibly have destroyed ourselves.

It is therefore important that a believer should learn to walk in the Spirit and develop and maintain a spiritual walk before he may begin to ask God for an enlarged and sensitive heart.

Moses prayed, *"Now therefore, I pray thee, if I have found favour in thy sight, show me now thy ways, that I may know thee and find favour in thy sight"* (Exodus 33:13). The Moses who could pray this was one who had walked with God, proved God, been proven by God and had found favour before the Lord. Moses could not have prayed that way in Egypt. In Egypt he did not have what it needed to pray like that. He was also not able to stand what would happen when such a prayer was answered.

Each believer must learn to make progress in walking with God. He must let the Cross put an end to his self life and he must let the Holy Spirit work out the formation of Christ within. Upon these would depend the extent of his fruitfulness in the ministry of praying for on these would depend the extent to which he can receive the will of God.

In this matter, there are practical things that a believer needs to do in order to co-operate with the Cross in the bringing of the self-life to an end as well as co-operating with the Holy Spirit for the formation of Christ within. There are three practical things. The apostle Paul sums these up in Colossians by saying, *"If then you have been raised with Christ, seek the things that are above, where Christ is seated at the right hand of God. Set your minds on things that are above, not on things that are on earth. For you have died, and your life is hid with Christ in God"* (Colossians 3:1-3). We can present this as follows:

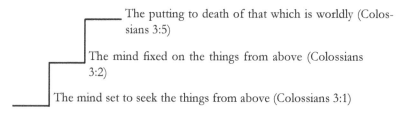

The putting to death of that which is worldly (Colossians 3:5)

The mind fixed on the things from above (Colossians 3:2)

The mind set to seek the things from above (Colossians 3:1)

A practical approach to the spiritual walk

Those who walk this way will maintain a spiritual walk. They will be spiritually normal. The apostle Paul continues to teach, *"Those who belong to Christ Jesus have crucified the flesh with its passions and desires"* (Galatians 5:24). *"If we live by the Spirit, let us also walk by the Spirit"* (Galatians 5:25).

One of the desires that must be put to death is talktativeness. None can make deep progress in knowing God's will and in prayer without that they have put their tongues under control. This is so because the tongue is an important organ in prayer. We know from hard-earned experience that one careless word of joking, jesting or anger can cause very heavy spiritual loss.

One other desire that needs to be curbed is the desire for human company. Those who would develop an intimate walk with God must increasingly sacrifice the company of man in order to seek Him. That is a real test of the sincerity of all who say that they want to know His will and then pray accordingly.

May I ask you a personal question: *"Where do you stand with regards to all this? Have you actively decided and acted on the command to seek the things above; set your mind on the things above, and to put to death what is earthly in you,"* If you have, praise the Lord! Continue to walk that way for it is a once and for all thing, a crisis, and a daily thing, a process. If you have not, today is the day to begin. This very minute is your time for action! Praise the Lord.

Part 3

PURITY OF HEART AND THE RECEPTION OF THE WILL OF GOD

16

•••••••

God the dwelling place of man

God made man for Himself. God made man to dwell in Him. Normally, man should dwell totally within God. God meant that, we should live and move and have our being in Him. The Psalmist wrote, *"Lord, thou hast been our dwelling place in all generations"* (Psalm 90:1); *"He who dwells in the shelter of the Most High, who abides in the shadow of the Almighty, will say to the Lord, My refuge and my fortress; my God in whom I trust"* (Psalm 91:1-2). The Lord said by the mouth of the prophet, Therefore say, *"Thus says the Lord God: Though I removed them far off among the nations, and though I scattered them among the countries, yet I have been a sanctuary to them for a while in the countries where they have gone"* (Ezekiel 11:16).

God has decided that man should be His dwelling place. The holiness of God makes it absolutely necessary that man be holy in order to comfortably dwell in God.

All believers dwell in the Lord, but not all believers dwell comfortably in God. Not all believers are at rest in the Lord. Some dwell in God as a man dwells in a strange house in which he longs to go out but is unable to depart.

The knowledge of the fact that you are dwelling in the Lord should cause you to tremble. It should cause you to depart from all sin. The apostle wrote, *"Let every one who names the name of the Lord depart from iniquity"* (2 Timothy 2:19). If those who name the name of the Lord must depart from iniquity, how much more should those who dwell in the God of all holiness? The Lord commands all to be holy for He is holy. No one dares to ignore that command.

You will not be able to fully receive the will of God if, because of sin, you cannot dwell in God as you ought. The way to normalize the situation is to part with sin for ever. Decide now that you and all that is sinful in your life will part company for ever. Do that and your heart will be rendered pure and then you will be able to receive the will of God. Do that because, since you are dwelling in God, you do Him great injustice to harbour any sin whatsoever.

A certain king once found a poor, wretched beggar and invited him to come and dwell in his palace. Before admitting the beggar into his palace, he took away his rags, dirty shoes and separated him from the dust bins from which he used to scavenge for food. He gave the man new and expensive clothes and gave him a place on his right hand at his table. The beggar was allowed to eat all that the king ate at any time and in any quantity. He was given a suite of rooms and limitless clothing, shoes and all else. He was told that he could have anything else that he wanted for the asking. The beggar felt at home for some time. Then he decided to go outside and bring the dustbin from which he used to seek food in the past. He installed it in the centre of the king's reception room. He went for his old rags and wore them over his new and expensive clothes and continued to install all that was of his past in the king's beautiful and clean palace. What do you think would happen to his relationship with the king?

Are you doing any of the things that the beggar did?

What has happened to your relationship with the King?

What has happened with your relationship with the One who gave Himself to be your dwelling place?

17

• • • • • • • •

Man : the dwelling place of God

God has always wanted to dwell in man. He yearns for that and longs for it. God dwelt in the Lord Jesus while He was on earth. The Lord Jesus said, *"Do you not believe that I am in the Father and the Father in me? The words that I say to you I do not speak on my own authority; but the Father who dwells in me does his works. Believe me that I am in the father and the Father in me; or else believe me for the sake of the works themselves"* (John 14:10-11). He continued to say, *"He who has my commandments and keeps them, he it is who loves me, and he who loves me will be loved by my Father, and I will love him and manifest myself to him."* Judas (not Iscariot) said to him, *"Lord, how is it that you will manifest yourself to us, and not to the world?"* Jesus answered him, *"If a man loves me, he will keep my word, and my Father will love him and we will come to him and make our home with him"* (John 14:21-23).

So the Father dwelt in the Son and the Father and Son seek those in whom They may come into and make their home in them. The fact that God the Father and God the Son desire to dwell in human beings is one of the greatest manifestations of God's love for man and also of God's deep humility. It is also a manifestation of the great extent to which God wants to exalt man. So, the door is open for any who want to have God dwell within them. Such have two requirements to fulfil. First of all they must have the commandments of the Lord Jesus. Secondly they must keep them. Any who fulfil these requirements will have the greatest thing that can happen on earth happen to them. God the Father would come along with God the Son (and certainly with God the Holy Spirit) and they will make their home in the person. This is most glorious - to become the home of God; to carry God with you wherever you go. To have God do everything you are doing with you! How glorious! How frightful! How awe inspiring - that a human being should carry deity within him!

Could God offer something greater to man? I do not think any offer of God can be greater. What it means is that God would become (and I write humbly and reverently) man's possession! This reminds me of what happened in the Old Testament. The Lord said to Aaron, *"You shall have no inheritance in their land, neither shall you have any portion among them; I am your portion and your inheritance among the people of Israel"* (Numbers 18:20). God did not limit it to Aaron. He extended it to the Levites. The Bible says, *"At that time the Lord set apart the tribe of Levi to carry the ark of the covenant of the Lord, to stand before the Lord to minister to him and to bless in his name, to this day. Therefore Levi has no portion or inheritance with his brothers; the Lord is his inheritance, as the Lord your God said to him"* (Deuteronomy 10:8-9). So, Aaron, his sons and the Levites had God as their portion and as their inheritance. God became their possession.

The consequences of God becoming man's possession are very far-reaching. First of all, it means that in a sense, man has not only God but also has all that God has! This means that the one indwelt by God is rich beyond measure. He is superabundantly supplied with all that God is and all that God has. This is deeply real but the eyes of the one who is indwelt by God have to be opened. To that end the apostle Paul prayed, *"Because I have heard of your faith in the Lord Jesus and your love towards all the saints, I do not cease to give thanks for you, remembering you in my prayers, that the God of our Lord Jesus Christ, the Father of glory, may give you a spirit of wisdom and of revelation in the knowledge of him, having the eyes of your hearts enlightened, that you may know what is the hope to which he has called you, what are the riches of his glorious inheritance in the saints, and what is the immeasurable greatness of his power in us who believe, according to the working of his great might"* (Ephesians 1:15-19). So, there is a real sense in which those who are now indwelt by God have everything that God has and lack absolutely nothing; There is a sense in which there is nothing that God can do to add to the possessions of the believer because, having given him Himself, He has given him (the believer) all that He has and having given all, there is nothing more that He can give.

There is also a sense in which the believer who is indwelt by God cannot lack nor desire anything because he has God and has all that God has and therefore all his needs have been supplied, for what does God not have and what is too hard for God?

INCREASING DWELLING

Although the believer has God for his possession; although he is indwelt by Him, there is need for 'increasing dwelling.' What do we mean? We mean that God must be allowed to dwell in the whole of man. He must be given right of access to every area of man. He must fully possess man in order that man may fully possess Him. He must own all of the man in whom He dwells so that the man in whom he dwells may own all of God and all that God has. Consequently, the believer owns and possesses God to the extent that he has allowed God to own and possess him. The ones who are totally possessed of God are also the ones who are most immeasurably rich.

It is this that makes increasing dwelling a necessity. That is why the apostle Paul wrote to the Ephesian believers, *"For this reason I bow my knees before the Father, from whom every family in heaven and on earth is named, that according to the riches of his glory he may grant you to be strengthened with might through his Spirit in the inner man, and that Christ may dwell in your hearts through faith; that you, being rooted and grounded in love, may have power to comprehend with all the saints what is the breath and length and height and depth, and to know the love of Christ which surpasses knowledge, that you may be filled with the fullness of God"* (Ephesians 3:14-19).

The purpose of increasing dwelling is that the believer may be filled with the fullness of God. This means that there are varying stages of His dwelling. It means that when He comes in He occupies what He is allowed to occupy. As more room is given to Him, He moves into the new area that is given to Him. Every area that He is given He fills with His fullness. When every area is given to Him, He fills every area with His fullness. The believer is then filled with the very fullness of God.

The purpose of God dwelling the believer is that the believer may be filled with the very fullness of God.

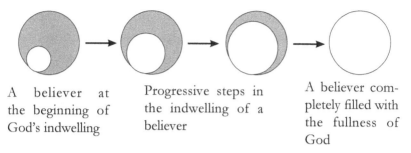

A believer at the beginning of God's indwelling

Progressive steps in the indwelling of a believer

A believer completely filled with the fullness of God

The increasing indwelling of God in the believer

The progressive indwelling of God in the heart of the believer is dependent on the degree of total surrender that the believer knows. The one who surrenders a part of himself completely will know the fullness in that part. The one who surrenders all of himself wholly will know fullness in all of his being.

MAN AS THE DWELLING PLACE OF GOD AND SIN

That God should come to dwell in man is an awesome thing. That man should have the liberty to carry God in him and go wherever he goes with God is most serious. This means that from the time that God comes into a believer, He is invited by the believer to fully become a part of his:

motives,

thoughts,

words, and

deeds.

This means that the believer who deliberately commits any sin however *"small"* in his thoughts, words or action is doing nothing less than trying to choke, strangle or kill the God within him.

The indwelling of God makes the abandonment of sin not only desirable but absolutely obligatory. YOU IN WHOM GOD DWELLS HAVE NO CHOICE WHATSOEVER BUT TO PART WITH EVERY SIN IN YOUR LIFE. Not to do that is to do God the greatest harm for it is an attempt to get Him to sin!

Since prayer is talking to the indwelling God, prayer is the function of people who have decided not to frustrate God's indwelling in them. This decision is made by radical and continuous departure from everything that is not worthy of God.

Purity then is a must.

Purity then is indispensable for a knowledge of God's will.

Now is the time of prayer.

Now is also the time for purity of heart.

18

•••••••

Communion between God and man

There is something better than occasional or frequent coming to the Lord for fellowship. Although God accepts and enjoys the times of fellowship that we grant to Him, He yearns for us. His *"frustration"* must be that we do not want something more than that.

There are some believers who have gone beyond having fellowship with God. Or to put it better, they have gone beyond having occasional fellowship with God. They have learnt to have communion with God.

There are two aspects to this. The first one is that of intimacy, of depth, of contact and of extension of contact. It is possible to shake a person's hand lightly. It is also possible to shake his hand firmly, so that the contact is firm and the grip total. There will thus be contact at the hands. It is also possible to go beyond a handshake to embrace a person lightly and briefly or to embrace him firmly and fully. Each of these will produce a different type of communication. This can be illustrated in the following Bible narrative, *"After this the son of the woman, the mistress of the house became ill; and his illness was so severe that there was no breath left in him. And she said to Elijah,"* What have you against me, O man of God? You have come to me to bring my sin to remembrance, and to cause the death of my son! *"And he said to her,"* Give me your son. *"And he took him from her bosom, and carried him up into the upper chamber, where he lodged, and laid him on his own bed. And he cried to the Lord,"* O Lord my God, hast thou brought calamity even the widow with whom I sojourn, by slaying her son? *"Then he stretched himself upon the child three times, and cried to the Lord,"* O Lord my God, let this child's soul come into him again. *"And the Lord hearkened to the voice of Elijah; and the soul of the child came into him again, and he revived"* (1 Kings 17:17-22).

Elisha was in a similar incident. The Bible says, *"When Elisha came into the house, he saw the child lying dead on his bed. So he went in and shut the door upon the two of them, and prayed to the Lord. Then he went up and lay upon the child, putting his mouth upon his mouth, his eyes upon his eyes, and his hands upon his hands; and as he stretched himself upon him, the flesh of the child became warm. Then he got up again, and walked once to and fro in the house, and went up and stretched himself upon him; the child sneezed seven times, and the child opened his eyes"* (2 Kings 4:32-35).

It can be seen that there was much contact between the prophets and the dead children. It is also obvious that the contact between Elisha and the dead child of the Shunamite was more intimate than that between Elijah and the other woman's child.

So it is possible to touch God superficially or intimately.

The other aspect (the second one) has to do with duration. There can be intimate but short-lived contact or there can be intimate and sustained contact. The Lord desires that there be intimate and sustained communion with Him. His desire is that we grow to such a place in our relationship with Him that we never depart from His presence. That means that our communion with Him is unceasing. It will mean that during times of *"active"* and *"passive"* prayer, we are in communion with Him.

Such communion has repercussions; First of all, it demands that God should be our greatest joy so that living unceasingly in His presence satisfies the deepest longing of our hearts. Secondly it means that other people and things have such a low priority in our lives that we shall not be yearning to depart from the presence of God and go to give them undivided attention. It means that even when we are giving someone attention, our communion with God remains deeply intact and we are continuously being led by the Lord on how to relate with the person. The third repercussion is that such communion cannot exist where there is the slightest sin or the slightest questionable practice. Those who come occasionally into God's presence can, like Israel of old, purity themselves and thereby prepare to come into His presence. They can labour to maintain their purity until they normal selves and to do what they want.

The person who, on the other hand, is living in unceasing communion with God does not have such lapses during which he can flirt with the questionable for a while. He is like Aaron in the Holy of holies. His dwelling place is in the Holy of holies, i.e. God's immediate presence. His contact is constantly with the God of all holiness. He must be holy not occasionally but all the time. The purity of heart is maintained round the clock. There is a real sense of the fear of the Lord upon him. Like Aaron of old, in the Holy of holies, he knows that there is no room at all for the slightest sin and the slightest departure from the Lord. All must just be correct and all must be correct all the time.

That is the type of life that the Lord invites His own to live in Him. From that kind of living flows unceasing prayer to the Lord; prayer that is after the counsel of God for that counsel is being received continuously. Such a person is like a waiter at table. If there is something needed, he knows at once and asks. If there is nothing, he just stays before the Lord, lost in worshipping and adoring him. This is wonderful. This is great.

How could believers run away from paying the price for such a life which is indeed heaven on earth? The answer lies in the heart. There are few, very few whose hearts have been truly circumcised to love the Lord and are actively loving Him. Such will enjoy unceasing communion and pay any price to enter and abide in it. May God make you into one such. You will then cry to God for such a heart and continue to cry until He gives you one. You will do all to maintain its purity. You will seek God and labour to know Him, love Him and live in His immediate presence. Then there will be quality in your prayer and quantity too and it will be rare that your prayer goes unheard. You will not pray primarily to have answers. You will pray to worship, adore and then answers will come as an overflow of your communion with God. Praise the Lord!

19
·········

God dwells in the believer's spirit

We know that man is tripartite. The Bible shows this in many passages but we shall cite just two of them to confirm the fact that man is tripartite4. *"Hear, O Israel. The Lord our God is one Lord; and you shall love the Lord your God with all your heart, and with all your soul, and with all your might (body)"* (Deuteronomy 6:4-5); *"May the God of peace himself sanctify you wholly; and may your spirit and soul and body be kept sound and blameless at the coming of our Lord Jesus Christ. He who calls you is faithful, and he will do it"* (1 Thessalonians 5:17).

Man thus has a spirit a soul and a body. With his spirit, man relates to the spirit world and with his body he relates to the physical world. The soul is between the spiritual and the physical.

The spirit of man has three parts or components or functions: the intuition, the conscience and the communion. The soul of man also has three parts or functions - the will, the mind and the emotions. The body again has three parts: the bones, the blood and the muscles. We can lay it out as follows:

The spirit
1. conscience
2. intuition
3. communion

The soul:
4. will
5. mind
6. emotion

The body
7. bones
8. blood
9. muscles

God is Spirit. He can only dwell in a spirit. The God heaven dwells in man's spirit in the person of the Holy Spirit. God dwells in the human spirit. He cannot dwell in the soul or in the body of man. The Holy Spirit does not come into direct contact with the soul and the body of man. He always reaches out to the soul through the spirit; and then indirectly through the spirit to the soul and through the soul to the body. We can illustrate this in two ways.

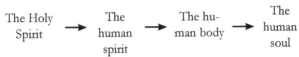

The Holy Spirit → The human spirit → The human body → The human soul

The sequence or impact of the Holy Spirit on the entire man

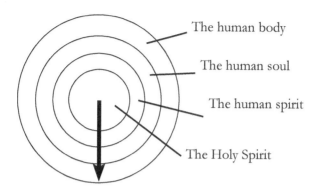

The Holy Spirit indwelling the human spirit and the direction of
its impact on the spirit, soul and body of man

The fact that the Holy Spirit dwells in the spirit of man means that sins of the heart become critically important. Impure thoughts, wicked thoughts, impure or wicked desires, pride in the heart, envy, discontentment, greed, covetousness, spite and every other sin that may be committed in the heart but not exteriorized becomes as harmful to spiritual progress as the sins that begin in the heart and go on to have an outward manifestation in the soul and body.

The believer who wants to pray knows then that if there is no purity of heart, he will not be able to receive the will of God as it should be received. He may be very intelligent and can grasp things clearly with his mind; he may have a fully developed will and well developed and well refined emotions. These cannot help him to receive God's will because it is imparted by the Holy Spirit directly on his spirit independent of the condition of his soul. The condition of his soul only matters in the secondary process of the transfer of that which is on the spirit to the soul. This means that any failures in the primary process of the Holy Spirit imparting to the human spirit cannot be corrected in the soul regardless of how developed it might be.

This being so, the priority of a believer is to keep his spirit pure. The purity that is acceptable is that which satisfies the heart of God. Man only sees the condition of the spirit of another indirectly. Consequently it is not primarily a matter of pleasing man. God's heart must be satisfied. It is satisfied by pleasing His Spirit that dwells in man.

Those who are serious with God and consequently serious about prayer and therefore serious about receiving the will of God will pay more attention to the condition of their spirit than a man pays to his eyes. The slightest uncongruency there produces disorder.

There is therefore no place for any form of hypocrisy whatsoever in the life of the praying believer! Hypocrisy is sin and sin means that prayer can no longer satisfy the heart of God.

Inward holiness then is a must.

God open the eyes of your children to see this.

Lord, open their inner eyes to respond accordingly.

Lord, deliver them from confusing mental analysis of facts with the Spirit's impartation of facts. Lord, grant discernment of that which is from the Holy Spirit and that which is from the outside. Lord grant that the knowledge will have spiritual repercussions in holiness and prayer! Lord, O for a deeper measure of it afresh in my inner man!

20

· · · · · · · ·

Engraving the image

We have shown clearly that true praying must begin in the heart of God. It is when a believer receives the will of God from the Father and prays it back to Him so that He may bring it to pass. We have shown the importance of purity of heart in the reception of God's will. In this chapter, we will look at the necessity of purity of heart for the proper engraving of the right image on the heart of man.

Sustained prayer implies that the will of God that is revealed to man will be received correctly and that the information that is received would be properly stored. Unless this is done how will a man be able to pray as he should?

This means that the heart of man must be in such a condition that all that the Lord reveals as His will will be correctly transmitted to man. Therefore what is on God's heart must be correctly engraved on the heart of man.

Let us look at a few example. If letters have been carved on a rubber stamp and ink applied to it, the rubber stamp can be stamped on a paper in order that what is on the rubber stamp will appear on the paper. If someone is to read what is on the paper and know what was on the rubber stamp, then the surface of the rubber stamp, the ink applied to it and the surface of the paper on which the stamping has to be done must be such that the entire image on the stamp would be correctly transferred to the paper. For our present purposes the stamp represents the will of God and the into will not be considered. We shall look at the heart of the believer and the engraving of the will of God on it.

If a rubber stamp is being engraved upon a surface, the letters on the stamp will appear correctly and clearly on the paper surface if the surface is even, untwisted and with no objects on it. A thin film of transparent material or of translucent material will prevent the image from being transferred from rubber stamp to paper. On the other hand, such obstacles may be absent, whereas what is present are small grains of sand particles. They will cause the surface of the paper to be uneven. The result of this is that some letters will appear clearly, others will appear but not be clear and others will not appear at all. The same thing will happen if the surface of the paper is twisted.

The particles on the paper represent anything on the heart of man that is not there by the perfect will of God. They could be particles of sin-deliberate disobedience. They could be particles of indulgence - excess food, sleep and the like. They could be the particles of independence from God which may represent projects that have their origin in the desires of man's heart and not in the heart of God. They could be the particles of the dead works of man - man's desire to please God by his projects that he conceived, determined how to do them and went about doing them sacrificially without seeking God's will from the start and throughout the operation. The particles could represent innocent things on the heart of man. They are not sinful. They only occupy space and are cumbersome and thus making it impossible for the Holy Spirit to have unhindered contact with the spirit of man.

The surface of the paper could be ruffled or twisted. Again such a surface will prevent the full image from being engraved on the spirit of the believer.

For the will of God to be clearly and completely imparted to the spirit of man, the spirit of man has to be normal. Things such as anxiety, worry, heaviness of spirit, distractions, pre-occupation with many things, lack of a capacity to concentrate, and so forth all contribute to reduce the capacity of the human spirit to receive the will of God in totality. We are not saying that God's will will, not be received at all. We are saying that God's will will not be received in totality. Is it a small thing that God should desire to impart the whole of His will to His child and the child should end up with only a part of it because of abnormalities in his spirit?

So there are two situations. One in which all of the will of God is received and the other one in which only a part of it is received.

If two believers wait before God and because of the difference in the condition in which their spirits are one receives the full will of God while the other only has a part of God's will engraved on his spirit, they will present varying with to God in prayer. We can represent these as follows:

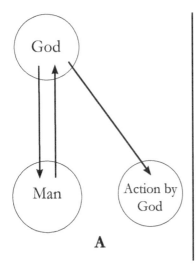

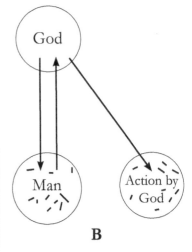

A pure spirit that allows the totality of God's will to be imparted to the spirit of man, resulting after prayer, in the carrying out of the full will of God

An impure spirit that receives only a part of God's will and leads to a partial action by God

When a believer prays, he will be bring to God the will of God that he received for action. He will be presenting what he received as his own will and pleading with God to take action. When the prayer gets to God, He will compare what has come back with what was His perfect will. If what gets back to Him is what He released, He will carry out action, that is, execute His full will. If what gets back is only a part of His will, He may decide not to act at all or to carry out action that corresponds to what He received back from man in prayer. This means that the acts of God in the world depend on the spiritual condition of those who pray. Some by their right spiritual condition co-operate with Him for the execution of His full and perfect will while others by the condition of their spirits cause Him to produce a work that is less than what His full purpose is.

That man has been allowed to influence what God produces is both fearful and frightful. It means that people should not only pray. They should also see what their spiritual conditions is like. In fact they should reflect on what their praying will enable God to produce. They should then come to a conclusion as to whether their praying will bless God and His purpose or not.

It could well mean that it would be better for some people not to pray at all. If a man would produce deformed children should he rather not reproduce? Should he not be encouraged to get healed before he reproduces? Similarly, there are people who should not pray or who should not be allowed to pray until they have become spiritually normal. To encourage everyone regardless of the condition of his heart to pray for God's interests is not spirituality but folly. God, set us free from that.

It is therefore better for a few people who are right with God to seek His will, know it and pray it through than for thousands of carnal believers who live in the indigence of the flesh to pray.

Those who are best able to receive the will of God are those who can pray the most effectively.

Again, we see that sin in any form and every other form of spiritual abnormalcy is a hindrance to prayer. May all His children take this seriously and work on it without delay and then, may they pray the entire will of God, thus giving God the opportunity to do His perfect will. Amen.

Part 4

BETWEEN REVELATION AND ASKING

21

....

Concretizing what has been received

When the will of the Lord has been communicated to a person, a great step in prayer has taken place. The person now has that which he can place before the Lord in prayer, knowing fully well that it is the will of God and insisting that it be done.

There is however one more problem. That which has been received can be forgotten. It can be snatched away by the enemy or the details can be lost. Everything should be done to ensure that what has been received is concretized.

The first thing that should be done is to thank the Lord for revealing His will. In thanking the Lord, what has been received is affirmed and thereby concretized.

The second thing is to protect that which has been received. The enemy once complained, *"Has thou not put a hedge about him and his house and all that he has, on every side?"* (Job 1:10). God put a hedge around Job and around Job's household and around all that Job had on every side. This hedge put Job, his household and all that he had out of reach of the enemy. The enemy saw him and his but could not attack because the hedge was in the way. Everything received from the Lord must immediately be protected from the enemy. By prayer, build a hedge around the will of God that you have just received, putting yourself and what you have received out of reach of the devil. When the revelation has thus been protected, there is safety.

The third thing that should be done to concretize it is to carry out preliminary praying about the Lord. We know from personal experience that after many hours of waiting before the Lord for His will to be received, when the revelation or confirmation does come there is either such joy or such relief that it is not easy to settle down to intercede or to supplicate. Although it is not easy, it should be done. The future could well depend on the fact that you discipline yourself for the next thirty minutes or one hour to bring that which you have received to the Lord in prayer.

We can learn something from king David. Immediately he was told that he was not to build the Lord a house but rather that the Lord would build him a house, the Bible says, *"Then King David went in and sat before the Lord, and said, Who am I, O Lord God, and what is my house, that thou hast brought me thus far? And this was a small thing in thy eyes, O God; thou hast also spoken of thy servant's house for a great while to come, and hast shown me future generations, O Lord God! And what more can David say to thee for honouring thy servant? For thou knowest thy servant. For thy servant's sake, O Lord, and according to thy own heart, thou hast wrought all this greatness, in making known all these great things. There is none like thee, O Lord, and there is no God besides thee, according to all that we have heard with our ears. What other nation on earth is like thy people Israel, whom God went to redeem to be his people, making for thyself a name for great and terrible things, in driving out nations before thy people whom thou didst redeem from Egypt? And thou didst make thy people Israel to be thy people for ever;*

and thou, O Lord, didst become their God. And now, O Lord, let the word which thou hast spoken concerning thy servant and concerning his house be established for ever, and do as thou hast spoken; and thy name will be established and magnified for ever, saying, 'The Lord of hosts, the God Israel, is Israel's God,' and the house of thy servant David will be established before thee. For thou, my God, hast revealed to thy servant that thou wilt build a house for him; therefore thy servant has found courage to pray before thee. And now, O Lord, thou art God, and thou hast promised this good thing to thy servant, now therefore may it please thee to bless the house of thy servant, that it may continue for ever before thee; for what thou O Lord, hast blessed is blessed for ever" (1 Chronicles 17:16-27).

David's first reaction was to pray. He was full of joy; he was overwhelmed but he brought his joy before the Lord and rejoiced in the Lord and before the Lord. He was deeply moved. He was overflowing and he found in God the closest companion with whom to share his moment of bliss.

This was because of a deep and intimate relationship built with the Lord over the years. God was first in his life. God was his closest friend, his most intimate lover and the one to whom he needed to break his greatest news before others could hear afterwards. Yes, he had built that relationship with the Lord before. It did not come with the revelation. Earlier on he had said, *"Whom have I in heaven but thee? And there is nothing upon earth that I desire besides thee"* (Psalm 73:25). He had also said before, *"O God, thou art my God, I seek thee, my soul thirsts for thee; my flesh faints for thee, as in a dry and weary land where no water is"* (Psalm 63:1). He had learned to love God and actually loved and was satisfied with God and in God. The result was that when he received the big news from God, he ran first into God's presence to share it with Him and to consolidate things with Him. He did and we thank God for it. We too must walk by the Spirit and know God. We must have Him as our exceeding great joy so that when He will give us a much needed revelation, we shall find His presence; we shall find him as the most logical person to first share with and as we do we shall concretize what we have received in His presence. Praise the Lord.

The last thing that should be done to concretize the revelation is to write it down. The Bible is the revealed will of God. The Lord caused the prophets to write down what He said to them. In this way the people could later turn to it, know God's will and know what to pray for and how to pray about it. There is a beautiful example given for us in Daniel. The Bible says, *"In the first year of Darius the son of Ahasuerus, by birth a Mede, who became king over the realm of the Chaldeans - in the first year of his reign, I, Daniel, perceived in the books the number of years which, according to the word of the Lord to Jeremiah the prophet, must pass before the end of the desolations of Jerusalem, namely, seventy years. Then I turned my face to the word of the Lord to Jeremiah the prophet, must pass before the end of the desolations of Jerusalem, namely, seventy years. Then I turned my face to the Lord God, seeking him by prayer and supplication with fasting and sackcloth and ashes. I prayed to the Lord my God and made confession, saying, O Lord, the great and terrible God, who keepest covenant and steadfast love with those who love him and keep his commandments..."* (Daniel 9:1-19). Had the prophet Jeremiah not written what the Lord revealed to him, it would have been impossible for Daniel to know about it, discern the timing and pray about it. Because it was written, it was preserved, and prayed through to accomplishment.

We too must write down what has been revealed to us as God's will. We must write it down in detail so that we shall be able to pray it through in detail until all of it has been accomplished. We dare not be lazy and deceive ourselves that we will remember it all for we shall not, remember all. If we do not write all we shall forget parts of it and then fill the gaps with our own imaginations and thus present to the Lord a distorted form of His will. We dare not take God so lightly as to do such a thing with the precious revelations of His will that He dares to give us. Let us write them down and let us do so as soon as they are received.

Another advantage that comes with writing them is that we shall be compelled to pray until the Lord answers. We shall be forced to read what would have been written and know that this is God's will that has not yet passed into fulfilment, and that wants for us to pray it to fulfilment. Unless we write it down, we shall soon forget and how sad that is. God, help me not to treat you with such contempt as to permit myself the misfortune of forgetting Your precious revelation. Lord, grant that none of Your children who reads this would permit himself such misfortune through indulgence.

Amen.

22

·······

Believing what has been revealed

We have shown that God's will is revealed in two ways: directly and indirectly. In direct revelation, He takes the initiative to show us what He wants. In indirect revelation we ask Him to show us His will about a certain matter or we present what we think to Him and ten receive His will about it. It does not really matter how we come to know His will. What matters is that we know it.

The fact that God's will has come to us may not solve all our problems. There is the important question of sorting act whether what we have is the will of God. Questions may often arise as to whether we heard God correctly; if the voice we heard was the voice of the Holy Spirit or our own spirit or even that of the Enemy. We may wonder if we are not just reacting to a need. We may wonder if we have not just conditioned ourselves to think that way. We may even wonder whether we are not just responding to the environment or if we are not thinking that way because of some frustration. We may wonder whether we are just reacting to someone or to something or we are truly convinced.

That such questions, thoughts and feelings come is not surprising. I have faced them again and again. They come even more when the will of God concerns us as individuals and concerns something of critical importance to us. The more desperate we are to be correct, the more confused we may become. What is the way out of this? How can we be sure that what we think has been revealed is actually a revelation of God's will?

My first suggestion is that you should first of all believe that it is God's will. You are God's child. The chances that it is your heavenly Father talking to you far outweigh the chances that it is the Enemy talking to you. If there is no sin being knowingly harboured the chances of Satan talking to you are greatly reduced although not totally eliminated. If you have asked God to reveal His will to you in a certain matter and you are truly open to do His will, regardless of what that will may be then you can believe that He is the One guiding you. He has committed Himself saying, *"What man of you, if his son asks him for bread, will give him a stone or if he asks for a fish, will give him a serpent? If you then, who are evil, know how to give good gifts to your children, how much more will your Father who is in heaven give good things to those who ask him?"* (Matthew 7:9-11). You will not ask for His will and He lets you have the devil's will.

My second suggestion is that you should ask Him to confirm that what you have is His will. Ask Him to confirm it but do not tell Him what He should do to confirm it. Do not cast lots. Do not place fleeces before Him. His best guidance is from inside, by the Holy Spirit witnessing to your spirit and not from outside! However, if you are a spiritual babe you may use fleeces but be careful! Gideon was not convinced by one experiment with the fleece. He needed two!

My third suggestion is that you should read the Word. Check and find out what the Scriptures say about the matter. The Holy Spirit who wrote the Bible as God's reference revelation will never give any revelation that conflicts with what is in the reference revelation (the Bible). You read what the Bible says, there will be increasing assurance that the matter is from the Lord (if it is from Him). If it is not from Him, you will find that it does not fit well into the Scriptures even when you try to squeeze it in. The will of God will come with increasing peace for the one who is walking in obedience. In fact, everything that disturbs your peace is unlikely to be the will of God unless you are living knowingly in sin. The Bible says, *"And let the peace of Christ rule in your hearts, to which indeed you were called in the one body. And be thankful"* (Colossians 3:15). Someone has said, *"Let the peace of Christ umpire in your hearts."* The umpire blows the whistle when something is wrong. If everything is going well, he does not blow his whistle. When we are dealing with what is the will of God, we will grow increasingly in peace about it. It is the heavenly Umpire (the Holy Spirit) saying, *"Go on My child. This thing is of me. Go on. Go on."* We should then go on.

Recently I have come through a situation in which today I was sure that it was the will of God and I committed myself to it and soon I was not sure that it was His will and I got out of it and soon I was back into it and soon I was out of it. This is the only issue in my life in which I have been through such forward and backward move for over one year. I have now come to rest about the matter. It stemmed from my wanting to do things out of proportion to my faith and knowledge of the Lord. It stemmed out of my trying to please God outwardly beyond the place where I am pleasing Him inwardly. It stemmed out of a desire to make a sacrifice that God was not asking of me. It stemmed out of a desire to buy God. I have learnt and I thank God for taking me through it and teaching me His way.

My fourth suggestion is that you should consult your most valued earthly companion. He could be your father, mother, wife, husband, friend, teacher or so. He knows you and will be helpful.

My fifth suggestion is you should consult your spiritual leader if you are still confused. He will help you.

My last suggestion is that even if there are still lingering traces of doubts you should move ahead believing it to be God's will. If after you have done all you can to discern His will you make a mistake, He will help you out of it. Do not postpone action indefinitely. Remember that if it is His will then He has revealed it to you so that you should pray it back to Him for execution. So do not wait indefinitely.

Believe and act!

Amen.

23

• • • • • • • •

Change or transformation of heart

It could be that the will of God will come to us as a shock! We may be expecting one thing and then He reveals His will to be something totally different. Take the example of Abraham and Isaac. God suddenly asked Abraham to go and sacrifice Isaac. What a shock it must have been to Abraham!

For very mature people, their commitment to God and the extent to which the Cross has brought the self-life to an end and the Holy Spirit built in the life of Christ means that there are hardly any demands of God that will shake them completely. They may not even be shaken. Their all may have been on the altar for a long time that all they would do would be to say with their Lord, *"Now is my soul troubled. And what shall I say? 'Father, save me from this hour?' No, for this purpose I have come to this hour. Father, glorify thy name?"* (John 12:27-28).

For immature believers, the will of God can be a hard blow. Take for example, a student whose desire is to go abroad and study and his whole being has been tuned in that direction for a long time. Then while praying the Lord says to him, *"I am sending you to go and witness for me in the village of X for three years. Forget about your plans for further studies."* This may greatly shake, or slightly shake the student depending on the degree of his consecration to the Lord.

If he is greatly shaken, he should not just recite words and say, *"Lord, I plead with You in the name of the Lord Jesus that You should send me to the village X to go and witness for You there for the next three years."* If he just speaks with his lips without the full involvement of his heart, he would not be praying. The best thing is for him to be honest with God and tell God what he feels. He should then ask the Lord to forgive him for having nursed or entertained hopes and expectations that were not the Lord's.

After confession his sin, he should ask the Lord to touch his heart so that he can whole-heartedly accept God's will. God will do it. It may be necessary to be delivered of some prejudices and the like. These should be sorted with the Lord in detail.

You may ask me why all this is necessary. It is necessary because there is a world of difference between two people praying the will of God through - one praying the will that he delights in and the other praying the will that he does not delight in. It is very difficult for anyone to have a sustained burden and wrestle unceasingly for that which he does not delight in. Because the best position for supplication or intercession is one where the heart, soul and body are all caught up with the supplication or intercession, those who pray should do all that they can to get to that position so that they can pray with their entire spirit, soul and body.

The Lord is willing to carry out the necessary change in the heart. He is willing to carry out the necessary transformation. Let us turn to Him and He will do it. Amen.

24
....

Believing that God is committed to his will

Prayer involves a man putting his all to ensure that the will of God is done. Prayer may cost a man everything; It may cost him his life, his wealth, his education and his all. If a man begins to pray for a pagan tribe and is praying from a modern town, he may end up in that pagan tribe in some remote forest, and to win them for the Lord. Prayer is very risky business. No one is the same after he has prayed. No one can remain uninvolved after prayer.

If prayer is to cost a man so much, it becomes necessary for him to be sure that God is committed to His will. The question is, "Might God somewhere along the line give up on His will? Might He somewhere along abandon it so that the person who committed himself and his all to it is stranded?

The second question is, *"If God is committed to His will, is He able to bring that will to pass? Could the forces of opposition not overcome Him and thus frustrate His desire to accomplish His will?"*

To both these questions, we say with full assurance that the believer has no cause for alarm. God is irrevocably committed to His will and God is not only able. He is not only willing, He will accomplish all He has willed. His Word is very clear about this. Look at the following Scriptures:

1. *"Remember the former things of old; for I am God, and there is none like me, declaring the end from the beginning and from ancient times things not yet done, saying, 'My counsel shall stand and I will accomplish all my purpose,' calling a bird of prey from the east, the man of my counsel from a far country. I have spoken, and I will bring it to pass; I have purposed, and I will do it"* (Isaiah 46:9-11).

2. The Lord of hosts has sworn: *"As I have planned, so shall it be, and as I have purposed, so shall it stand"* (Isaiah 14:24).

3. *"For the Lord of hosts has purposed, and who will annul it? His hand is stretched out and who will turn it back?"* (Isaiah 14:27).

4. *"I am God, and henceforth I am He; there is none who can deliver from my and; I work and who can hinder it"* (Isaiah 43:13).

5. Behold, he snatches away; who can hinder? Who will say to him, *'What does thou?'* (Job 9:12).

6. *"O Lord, God of our fathers, art thou not God in heaven? Does thou not rule over the kingdoms of the nations? In thy hand are power and might, so that none is able to withstand thee"* (2 Chronicles 20:6).

7. *"I know that thou canst do all things, and that no purpose of thine can be thwarted"* (Job 42:2).

8. *"No wisdom, no understanding, no counsel, can avail against the Lord. The horse is made ready for battle, but the victory belongs to the Lord"* (Proverbs 21:30-31).

9. *"Be broken, you peoples, and be dismayed; give ear, all you far countries; gird yourselves and be dismayed; gird yourselves and be dismayed. Take counsel together, but it will come to nought;*

speak a word, but it will not stand, for God is with us" (Isaiah 8:9-10).

From these Scripture passages, it is obvious that God is committed to His will; that He has the power to accomplish His will and that He will accomplish all His will. The believer who receives His will by revelation has received that which must come to pass. Such a one can commit himself and his all to the will of God, fully assured that it will come to pass. Praise the Lord.

25

· · · · · · · ·

Believing that God will answer prayer

Now you know that God will accomplish His purposes. You know that He will not fail. There is one last question that may be coming up in your mind. The question is, *"Will God answer prayer? Can you pray in the centre of His will and be sure that you will be heard? Can you pray His will back to Him fully persuaded that when that will comes back He will answer?"* To all these questions we say one billion times, *"yes"*. He will answer. The whole Bible is full of promises that He will answer prayer that comes from those who are rightly related to Him. Look at the following promises and believe Him and His proclamations.

1. *"And this is the confidence that we have in him, that if we ask anything according to his will he hears us. And if we know that he hears us in whatever we ask, we know that we have obtained the requests made of him"* (1 John 5:14-15).

2. *"Elijah was a man of like nature with ourselves and he prayed fervently that it might not rain, and for three years and six months it did not rain on the earth. Then he prayed again and the heaven gave rain, and the earth brought forth its fruit"* (James 5:17-18).

3. *"Whatever you ask in my name, I will do it, that the Father may be glorified in the Son; if you ask anything in my name, I will do it"* (John 14:13-14).

4. *"If you abide in me, and my words abide in you, ask whatever you will, and it shall be done for you"* (John 15:7).

5. *"You did not choose me, but I chose you and appointed you that you should go and bear fruit and that your fruit should abide; so that whatever you ask the Father in my name, he may give it to you"* (John 15:16).

6. *"In that day you will ask nothing of me; Truly, truly, I say to you, if you ask anything of the Father, he will give it to you in my name. Hitherto you have asked nothing in my name; ask, and you will receive, that your joy may be full"* (John 16:23-24).

7. *"And will not God vindicate his elect, who cry to him day and night? Will he delay long over them? I tell you, he will vindicate them speedily"* (Luke 18:1-8).

8. *"And I tell you, Ask, and it will be given you; seek and you will find; knock, and it will be opened to you. For every one who asks receives, and he who seeks finds, and to him who knocks it will be opened"* (Luke 11:9-10).

9. *"Therefore I tell you, whatever you ask in prayer, believe that you have received it, and it will be yours"* (Mark 11:24).

10. *"Ask, and it will be given you; seek, and you will find; knock, and it will be opened to you. For every one who asks receives, and he who seeks finds, and to him who knocks it will be opened"* (Matthew 7:7-8).

The evidence is overwhelming. One could add to this the testimonies of people of Bible times who prayed and God answered them. One could add to it the testimonies of believers of post-Biblical times who prayed and God answered them. I could add to it my 50.000 recorded answers to prayers during the last ten years. There is not the slightest doubt that God answers prayers. He cannot fail at all. He ordained prayer as a means to accomplishing His purposes. As long as He is working out His purposes, it is impossible for Him to leave aside one of the chief methods that He is using to bring His purposes to pass.

WHAT IF GOD SHOULD MAKE AN EXCEPTION OF YOU?

You may agree that God's commitment to answer prayer is obvious and that He has answered the prayers of many of His children from time immemorial until this day. You may still think and say, *"Does God not have His favorites? Maybe I am not one of them. Maybe I do not fit in."*

Listen, dear one, God has no favorites. He has invited everyone who knows and loves Him to pray. If you know and love Him then you qualify. He even goes out of His way to answer the prayers of people before they have come to Him. How much more will He answer your prayer, you who is His child?

He yearns to accomplish His will through the prayers of His own. Will He leave a part of His will unaccomplished so as to show you disfavour? Certainly not. He will not do it. He will answer you. His promises say, *"For every one who asks receives, and he who seeks finds and to him who knocks it will be opened."* You are included. You are included. You are included. Doubt no more. Rather move ahead with full assurance and pray. Amen.

26

· · · · · · · ·

Burden: what it is

In normal speech, burden is a weight of some kind. It is something carried. It is something heavy. It is something uncomfortable. It is something one would like to get rid of.

What applies in normal speech as describing burden also applies to spiritual burdens. Let us look at a few people in the Bible who were burdened.

ABRAHAM WAS BURDENED BY HIS CHILDLESSNESS

Abraham was burdened by his childlessness. He therefore raised the matter with God whenever he could. The Bible says, After these things the word of the Lord came to Abrah in a vision, *"Fear not, Abram, I am your shield; your reward shall be very great"* (Genesis 15:1). If Abraham were not burdened,he would have accepted the promise and rejoiced about it. However, he was a man with a burden. The weight of childlessness was upon him and he would not be silent. He would not be satisfied with general promises about God being his shield and his reward being very great. He was burdened and spoke as if to say to God, *"I have a problem, a weight that is crushing me."* The Bible says, *"But Abram said, O Lord God, what wilt thou give me, for I*

continue childless, and the heir of my house is Eliezer of Damascus?"
And Abram said, *"Behold, thou hast given me no offspring; and
a slave born in my house will be my heir"* (Genesis 15:2-3). The
Lord spoke to ease his burden. He said to him, *"This man shall
not be your heir; your own son shall be your heir."* God did not
only speak. He tried to assure Abram. The Bible says, *"And
he brought him outside and said, Look toward heaven, and number
the stars, if you are able to number them."* Then he said to him,
"So shall your descendants be." Abram responded from the heart
to what the Lord had said. The Bible says, *"And he believed the
Lord; and he reckoned it to him as righteousness"* (Genesis 15:6).

Although Abram believed God the burden remained. He
then decided to have the burden discharged by doing something
about it himself instead of waiting on God. He listened to his
wife and went into Hagar, got a son with her and was relieved
of his burden. He was so relieved of his burden that he was
not prepared to exercise faith any more. There was no need
for faith. The burden was gone and with it the faith. The Bible
says, *"And God said to Abraham,"* As for Sarai your wife, you
shall not call her name Sarai, but Sarah shall be her name. I will
bless her, and moreover I will give you a son by her; I will bless
her, and she shall be a mother of nations; kings of people shall
come from her. *"Then Abrham fell on his face and laughed, and
said to himself,"* Shall a child be born to a man who is a hundred
years old? Shall Sarah, who is ninety years old, bear a child?
"And Abraham said to God, O that Ishmael might live in thy sight!"
(Genesis 17:15-18).

Three things could happen to a man under a burden. (1)
He may continue to look to God for God's timing and God's
way of discharging the burden and therefore continue to bear
the every-increasing burden. This is the pathway that ought to

be followed by those who are spiritually normal. (2) He may seek his own way of discharging the burden, discharge it and thus get rid of it. (3) He may stop walking with the Lord, stop exercising faith, stop looking to the Lord and then fill himself with other things and thus cause the burden to vanish.

PAUL WAS UNDER A BURDEN ABOUT THE SALVATION OF ISRAEL

Paul was under a burden over the salvation of Israel. He put it this way, *"I am speaking the truth in Christ, I am not lying; my conscience bears me witness in the Holy Spirit, that I have great sorrow and unceasing anguish in my heart. For I could wish that I myself were accursed and out off from Christ for the sake of my brethren, my kinsmen by race. They are Israelites, and to them belong the sonship, the glory, the covenants, the giving of the law, the worship, and the promises"* (Romans 9:1-4). Great anguish! Great sorrow! Unceasing anguish! Unceasing sorrow of heart! These are the materials of which real burden is made. That burden led to prayer. He said, *"Brethren, my heart's desire and prayer to God for them is that they may be saved"* (Romans 10:1).

Paul walked close to the Lord. He did not look for his own method of discharging his burden. The burden grew and possessed him so much that he was prepared to be accursed so that the burden might be discharged by Israel being saved. The burden therefore did not leave him undischarged God's way. It stayed with him. It was unceasing. It brought great sorrow. It caused a yearning and great desire of heart. He was prepared to pay any price for the burden to be discharged God's way.

HEZEKIAH HAD A BURDEN BECAUSE DEATH WAS UPON HIM

The Bible says, *"In those days Hezekiah became sick and was at the point of death. And Isaiah the prophet the son of Amoz came to him, and said to him, 'Thus says the Lord,' Set your house in order; for you shall die, you shall not reaver.' Then Hezekiah turned his face to the wall, and prayed to the Lord, saying, Remember now, O Lord, I beseech thee, how I have walked before thee in faithfulness and with a whole heart, and have done what is good in thy sight. And Hezekiah wept bitterly"* (2 Kings 20:1-3). He received revelation about God's will. It resulted in a burden and he responded by prayer.

HANNAH WAS BURDENED BY HER BARRENNESS

Hannah had no child. Her rival used to provoke her sorely to irritate her, because the Lord had closed her womb. *"So it went on year by year; as often as she went up to the house of the Lord, she used to provoke her. Therefore Hannah wept and would not eat. And Elkanah, her husband, said to her,"* Hannah, why do you weep? And why do you not eat? And why is your heart sad? Am I not more to you than ten son? After they had eaten and drunk in Shiloh, Hannah rose. Now Eli the priest was sitting on the seat beside the doorpost of the temple of the Lord. She was deeply distressed and prayed to the Lord, and wept bitterly. And she vowed a vow and said, *"O Lord of hosts, if thou wilt indeed look on the affliction of thy maidservant, and remember me, and not forget thy maidservant, but wilt give to thy maidservant a son, then I will give him to the Lord all the days of his life, and no razor shall touch his head."*

As she continued praying before the Lord, Eli observed her mouth. Hannah was speaking in her heart; only her lips moved, and her voice was not heard; therefore Eli took her to be a drunken woman. And Eli said to her, *"How long will you be drunken? Put away your wine from you."* But Hannah answered, *"No, my lord, I am a woman sorely troubled; I have drunk neither wine nor strong drink, but I have been pouring out my soul before the Lord. Do not regard your maidservant as a base woman, for all along I have been speaking out of my great anxiety and vexation"* (1 Samuel 1:7-16).

Hannah was burdened. She reacted to the burden by fasting, praying and vowing. She continued with the burden until the priest's word brought hope and release.

WHAT THEN IS BURDEN?

"Burden is that restlessness, dissatisfaction with all else; that inner agitation in the spirit; that deep longing to see the revelation pass into fulfilment. Burden is something like a very heavy weight that rests on the heart of the person who has received a revelation of what God's need is or what God wants to bring to pass. Burden is something very much "alive". It can grow if well fed, it can shrivel if ill-fed and it can be starved to death. Burden that develops normally will lead to action. The action will first of all be prayer although it could be followed by other actions."

Revelation should lead to burden. What happens after that will depend on what the revelation was; what the burden was and what has happened to the burden after it was received. Praise the Lord.

27

·········

Faith and burden

The Bible says that without faith it is impossible to please God. Faith is an important ingredient in everything spiritual. Burden cannot exist without faith and without faith burden cannot grow. In fact, without faith burden dies. How is that so?

It is so, because faith enables a person to keep believing God. Faith enables him to initially lay hold on the revelation of God's need or the revelation of what God wants to do. As the person grows in faith so does his grip on the revelation grow. As he grows in faith so does his focus on the revelation grow. As he grows in faith so does his capacity to discern the different aspects of the burden.

Let us take the example of Paul. He said that he had great sorrow and unceasing anguish. He had unceasing burden. This was also because he had an unceasing faith that God would do something special for the salvation of his kinsmen, the Israelites. He manifested this unceasing faith by writing, *"I ask, then, has God rejected his people? By no means! I myself am an Israelite, a descendant of Abraham, a member of the tribe of Benjamin. God has not rejected his people whom he foreknew. Do you know what the Scripture says of Elijah, how he pleads with God against Israel?"* Lord, they have killed thy prophets, they have demolished thy altars, and I alone am left, and they seek my life. *"But what is God's reply to him?* "I have kept for myself seven thousand men who have not bowed the knee to Baal. *"So too at the present time there is a remnant, chosen by grace"* (Romans 11:1-5). He continued, *"Lest you be wise in your own conceits, I want you to understand this mystery, brethren: a hardening has come upon part of Israel, until the full number of the Gentiles come in, and so all Israel will be saved; as it is written, The Deliverer will come from Zion, he will banish ungodliness from Jacob; and this will be my covenant with them when I take away their sins. As regards the gospel they are enemies of God, for your sake; but as regards election they are beloved for the sake of their forefathers. For the gifts and the call of God are irrevocable"* (Romans 11:25-29).

As long as Paul believed that all Israel would be saved, his burden remained. And as long as he did something for the salvation of Israel, the burden grew. Paul did do something always for the salvation of the Jews. First of all, he always went to the synagogue first in each town along his missionary journeys. He tried to reach out to them. Even when they rejected him and he said that he was turning henceforth to the Gentiles, he did not reject them from his heart. He bore them in it and prayed unceasingly for them. So he kept having faith that what God promised would be realized and he continued doing something about it. He continued to pray and thus kept the burden growing and having an increasing grip of him.

BURDEN AND ASSURANCE OF FULFILMENT

Faith is the assurance of things hoped for. So, when we write about burden and assurance we are continuing to write about burden and faith. For burden to continue to lay hold of

and weigh increasingly on a man, he must have the unshakable
assurance that that burden would be discharged one day
and that in its being discharged, God's will that has indeed
become the person's will will be done. It is this unmistakable,
unshakable assurance that keeps the burden on and growing
during the various stages through which faith passes, namely:

1. the birth of faith
2. the growth of faith
3. the maturation of faith
4. the trials of faith
5. the battles of faith
6. the triumph of faith
7. the fulfilment of faith.

We can also talk of:

1. the birth of burden
2. the growth of burden
3. the maturation of burden
4. the trials of burden
5. the battles of burden
6. the triumphs of burden
7. the discharge of burden.

Lord, grant that Your children would *"see"* these things, be
given faith to grasp them, possess them, experience them and
consequently mature in the things that pertain to inner growth.

Amen.

28

....

Faith, burden, prayer and the goal of life

It is not possible to have faith in the Lord for everything. Faith requires concentration. It is also not possible to receive a burden for everything. Burdens need to be concentrated. It is also not possible to pray for everything. There is need for concentration in prayer.

If a person begins to pray for one thing and then moves quickly to another thing and then to a third, fourth and fifth, he may pray for one thousand things in one hour. He has actually perhaps not prayed but tossed a thousand things into the air and imagined that he has prayed. If this is not to be the case with us, we must have specific areas of concentration in prayer. We will of course pray for some general issues but we will concentrate on some specific thing or things.

How can we decide what we are to concentrate on? The answer is that the Lord will lead us as to what to concentrate on. What we shall concentrate on shall often be tied to the call of God on our lives and the goal that He has set before us. The goal will result in a burden to see it accomplished and that burden will force us to take no rest and give God no rest until it has happened.

We shall need faith to ask God to show us the one thing or the things He has called us to do for Him. We shall need faith to believe Him when He has spoken to us. We shall need to believe that we are able to do what he has called us to do for Him. We shall need faith to believe that we shall actually accomplish what He has called us to do for Him. We shall need faith to believe that the burden on our hearts will not evaporate before we have accomplished God's purpose and what God has committed to us. We shall need faith to pray; faith to keep praying, faith when prayers are not answered quickly and faith when the heavens seem sealed. We shall need faith when we fail and the Enemy says to us, *"It is finished. You have failed. Forget it. Do not make another attempt because the failure will even be greater."* We shall need faith to silence him, take up courage, forget the past and press on towards the goal. So faith is the environment in which the goal, burden and prayer dwell. It is the environment in which the burden dwell and is thereby not lost. It is the environment in which prayer is conceived, birthed, developed, matured and accomplished. We can illustrate these things as follows :

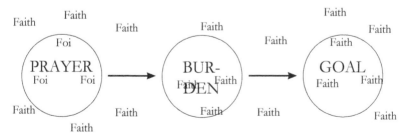

The relationship between faith, burden, prayer and the goal of life.

WHAT DOES THIS MEAN IN PRACTICE?

It simply means that before a person has received the call of God on his life and determined the goal that is to be accomplished by his obedience to the call of God, he should pray generally and move from one subject to the other as he likes. However, after he has received the call of God on his life, he is to concentrate his prayers in that direction. He will not stop praying for the other things, but he will concentrate on that to which the Lord has called him and by so doing he will concentrate on the burden to accomplish the goal of his life and the burden to pray. I cannot tell anyone how much time he will invest in praying for the goal of his life to be accomplished and how much time he will give to other things. It maybe that he might invest 75% of his praying into the goal of his life. It could be 70% or 60% or 50%. One thing is imperative - he will invest a significant portion of his praying into the goal of his life. This will cause burden for the accomplishment of the goal of his life to grow and also cause burden for prayer to grow. All this will lead to growth which may mean that he might increasingly give more and more time to praying for the accomplishment of the goal of his life as he gives more and more time to other things that would cause the goal to be accomplishment.

My prayer is that an increasing number of believers will have faith to ask, receive and labour to accomplish the goal that God has set for their lives. When this is done, the quality and the quantity of prayer will increase; the kingdom of God will advance; the devil and his kingdom will suffer loss; the Lord's heart will be satisfied and the believer will grow, be edified, and fulfilled. Glory be to the Lord. Amen.

29
•••••••

The development of burden

We have said that burden is a *"living"* thing. It can become stagnant; it can grow or it can die. The question that each person who wants to pray may want to ask is how he can develop the burden that is on his heart.

THERE MAY BE NO BURDEN TO BEGIN WITH

It should not be presumed that a knowledge of God's will will automatically and immediately lead to burden. There can be a knowledge of God's will that does not lead to burden. What should a person do in that situation? We recommend that he should use his mind and begin to pray on the things that he has received. If the Lord has shown him that He wants a particular person reached with the gospel, he should take over and begin to pray that that person will be reached. As he prays the salvation of that person will begin to weigh on him. As he prays more and more, the burden will grow. However, it is possible that even with more prayer a person may not have any burden apart from the fact that God wants a thing done. He should all the same continue to pray about it. God is not looking for our burden. He is waiting for our prayers. Therefore, the person who prays when he is burdened and who also prays when he is not burdened will make more progress. It should be realized that although revelation will normally lead to burden, no one is asked by the Lord to wait until he is burdened before he can pray. There is the matter of obeying the Lord. The kingdom of the enemy is never in greater danger than when a man decides that regardless of what he feels inside, he will obey the Lord. This obedience which may be unemotional will always do harm to the kingdom of Satan. This is because some people confuse burden with the emotions of their soul and may think that unless they feel like they should not pray. Every response in prayer contributes to bring glory to the Father and that contribution should always be made.

BURDEN COMES WITH OBEDIENCE

Although on some rare occasions prayer may not lead to burden, normally prayer leads to burden. The best way to develop burden is by prayer. When the will of God is received by revelation in the spirit of man, it would normally be communicated to the mind of man. As the mind receives the information, it will transmit it to the will. The man therefore wills that he would bring the will of God which he has received to accomplishment through prayer. The person who thus decides will begin to pray. He will pray even when he feels *"dry"* and *"empty."* He will continue to pray and as he prays he will begin to inwardly respond to the need of God. As he responds, first slowly and then increasingly, the burden will increase. We can illustrate it as follows:

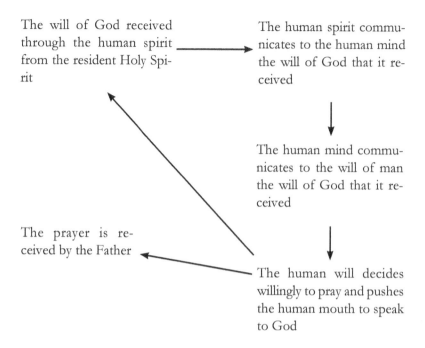

The will of God received through the human spirit from the resident Holy Spirit → The human spirit communicates to the human mind the will of God that it received ↓ The human mind communicates to the will of man the will of God that it received ↓ The human will decides willingly to pray and pushes the human mouth to speak to God → The prayer is received by the Father → The will of God received through the human spirit from the resident Holy Spirit

*As a person prays there is a feedback to the human spirit. This feedback contributes to the burden that forms in the human spirit about the issue being prayed about. The result is that the more a person prays about a thing, the more the burden grows and the more the burden grows the more the person will pray. It becomes obvious then that burden is proportional both to revelation and to prayer.

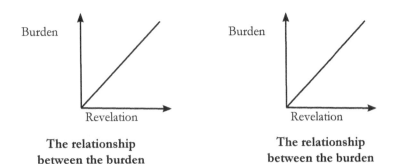

**The relationship
between the burden
and revelation**

**The relationship
between the burden
and prayer**

*The relationship between burden the relationship between burden and
revelation. and prayer. burden grows with holiness*

The environment in which relationships with the Lord
develop properly is that of holiness. There are three aspects
to this. First of all there is the aspect of separation from sin;
of deliverance from sin and self. In this it is obvious that the
person who separates himself more from sin will walk more
closely to the Lord. As he walks more closely to the Lord,
he will know and receive more of the burden that is on the
Lord's heart than the person who indulges occasionally in
sin. Secondly, there is the aspect of holiness that has to do
with being set aside for God's exclusive use. The person who
separates himself increasingly unto God and unto God's
exclusive use will spend more time in the immediate presence
of the Lord. Out of that time spent in the immediate presence
of the Lord will grow deeper communion with the Lord
and consequently greater impartation of the burden of the
Lord. First of all there will be more burden imparted initially.
Secondly the burden imparted will grow faster. Thirdly, there
is that aspect of holiness that has to do with the putting on
of the character of Christ. Those who have put on more
of Christ are able to receive more burden and what they are

provides an environment in which the burden can grow faster. We therefore say that burden grows in proportion to the extent to which a person has been delivered from sin and self and to the extent to which the person has separated himself unto God and put on Christ.

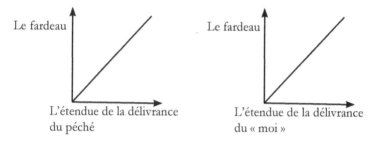

The relationship between the burden and the extent to which burden and the extent to which a person is delivered from sin. a person is delivered from self.

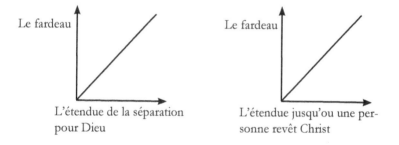

The relationship between the growth of burden and the extent growth of burden and the extent to which a person separates to which a person puts on christ. himself unto god. burden grows with spiritual nourishment

Because burden is living, if it is properly nourished, it will grow but if it is poorly nourished, it will weaken and decrease in size and finally die or disappear. The best way to nourish the burden is to read the word of God. The more a person reads the word prayerfully, the more the burden will be nourished and the more it will grow. In addition to reading the Bible, the person who wants his burden to grow should read books that will stimulate faith in the Lord. The person who grows in faith will also grow in burden. I have found that reading the biographies of people who spent and were spent in the service of the Lord and as a result of that did great things for Him, does challenge me to be my best for Him and in this way my burden to see an aspect of God's will materialize grows. As it grows I am able to press on and on in prayer. We can put it as follows:

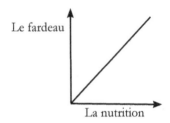

The relationship between the growth of burden and spiritual nourishment. burden grows with spiritual environment

The person who wants the burden he has to row must ensure that he lives in the right spiritual environment. He will be careful to ensure that he does not allow people who have no faith to come close to him. He will surround himself with people who believe God and speak the language of faith. He will surround himself with people who pray and who are committed to seeing the will of God become reality. So the burden will grow tilth the spiritual environment in which the person lives.

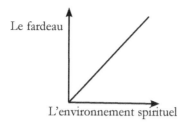

The relationship between the growth of burden and the right spiritual environment.

Part 5

THE DISCHARGE OF BURDEN

30
••••••••

General issues - 1

The burden of God on a heart or the revelation received will issue in prayer depending on what happens to the heart on the reception of the revelation or burden. What happens will depend on what type of heart is involved. We can illustrate it diagramatically as follows:

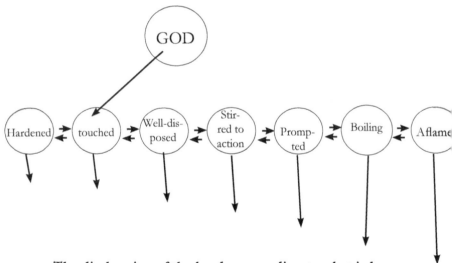

The discharging of the burden according to what is happening in the heart after revelation or burden has been received

When the Lord touches a heart and reveals the burden on His heart to that one, the extent to which the person will react will depend on what happens to the heart after the burden has been received. It is possible that the person receives the revelation but does not respond to the Lord. In that case the heart that was initially touched will become hardened. If the heart is hardened then there will be no discharge of burden. That means that the person will not pray at all. If that happens then the burden has been put to nought and the purpose of God hindered.

On the other hand the heart that is touched may respond in prayer immediately and thus discharge the burden that it has received, and not bother any more. The burden has thus been discharged at the stage *"touched."* Because there was no further development in the heart after the burden was received, the burden discharged is on a small scale.

It is possible, on the other hand that the heart that is touched receives the burden and determines not to discharge it at once but rather, by seeking God further and crying out to God for expansion and transformation is changed into a heart that is willing. The heart that is willing will discharge the burden to a greater extent than if the burden had been discharged at the stage *"touched."* On the other hand, the burden may be maintained and the Lord sought further so that the willing heart is transformed into a heart that is *"moved."* It could then discharge the burden or bear the burden and press on for more of what will convert it into a heart that is *"shined."* It may then discharge its burden or by the same process press on until it is a heart aflame. The heart that is aflamed will discharge the burden that it has received to the greatest extent possible for the human heart.

It should be noticed that the person concerned has a choice as to whether the burden will be discharged at any of the afore-mentioned stages. To carry a burden while dore for the heart to be transformed from one stage to the other is not easy. It demands dwelling in God's presence. It demands heart-cries and heart-searches. It demands pleading with God that the burden will be preserved from discharge until the heart is in the condition in which it can do the greatest discharge. It is like a woman who labours to ensure that the baby is not born before term. It is like a farmer who labours to ensure that his crops reach maturity before harvest for he knows that the best prices are obtained only for those crops that are fully mature.

The question may be asked why one needs to bear the burden and suffer the discomfort of carrying a burden while are with God to have his heart condition changed for the better. To answer this question we say that if it purely a personal matter. There are some who feel that provided the burden is discharged, they would be satisfied and not bother about the quality of discharge. There are, however, others who feel that God deserves the best and that they would not offer anything to the Lord without ensuring that they have done all that they could do to improve its quality to the maximum possible. It is these who believe in giving God their utmost best that will languish with the burden until their hearts are such as can discharge all of it to the father's satisfaction. May God raise many of this kind in His Body today. May God impart to His a dislike of all that is less than the best. May He give to His love of perfection so that this will put an end to mediocrity in prayer. Amen.

The other matter is that the heart condition touched, willing, moved, etc. vary from person to person, depending on his spiritual growth, sacrifice, consecration and experience. The heart aflame of a mature, consecrated believer will discharge burden to a far greater extent than that of the heart of an immature but consecrated believer.

It is imperative then that the believer should learn how to prevent pre-mature discharge of burden. He should also learn how to *"block"* the burden from recession to a lower stage in his labour to move it to a higher condition. He must learn how to consolidate the burden in a certain stage without discharging it. These are some of the lessons to be learnt in prayer.

31

......

General issues - 2

Although what we have said in the previous chapter is true and is in reality what takes place in most believers and in most situations, there is another situation where God moves directly on the heart, depending upon what type of heart it is and what that person has done with the burden, to ensure that there is the discharge of burden. What is discharged in prayer then will vary from heart to heart. It will also vary with impact. We illustrate it as follows:

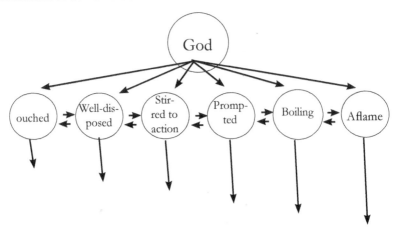

The discharge of burden of various hearts in response to the direct touch of God. the length of arrow indicates magnitude of impact of prayer.

In this situation, the extent to which the burden is discharged does not depend on what happens to the heart after the burden has been received but on what the heart was before the burden was received. In this case, the heart discharges the burden immediately it is received. God moves on the heart in proportion to what it is. He places the quantity and quality of burden on a heart that corresponds to what the heart is. The heart then receives only the burden that it is able to immediately discharge. This means that the more prepared a heart is the more burden it will receive and the more burden it receives the more burden it will discharge.

This being so, we say that God gives to each one burden that corresponds to what his heart is like. To the heart that is *"touched"* corresponding burden is given and to the heart that is willing, corresponding burden is given, and so on.

This places real importance on what a man's whole life is before God and not the aspect of his life as touches prayer. It brings to mind the fact that one who wants to make progress in the prayer life must make progress in every aspect of his walk with God. He cannot ignore other demands of Christ like character: humility, love, joy, patience and others, and decide that he will pray and thus solve every problem.

What does it mean for a heart to be touched, willing, moved, stirred, burning and aflame? We shall look at this in the following chapters.

32

....

A heart touched

When a person receives a revelation or a burden, his heart is touched. God is the one who touches hearts. The Bible says, *"Saul also went to his home at Gibeah, and with him went men of valour whose hearts God had touched. But some worthless fellows said,"* How can this man save us? *"And they despised him and brought him no present"* 1 Samuel 10:26).

A heart that is touched can resist what God is saying. In that case it becomes hardened or it could discharge its burden and be converted into a willing heart.

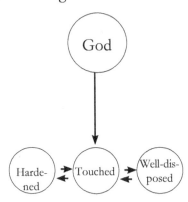

A heart that is touched can discharge its burden immediately, or it could become a willing or hardened heart. A hardened heart can be changed into a touched heart if there is repentance.

A touched heart can become a willing heart by further seeking of the Lord.

There could be various kinds of touches depending upon the intimacy of contact between a believer's spirit and the Holy Spirit. As a person grows deeper in fellowship with the Holy Spirit, the touches will become lighter. This is because the Holy Spirit expects more sensitivity and more receptivity from the spirit that has known sustained fellowship with God. Normally, God only speaks in hard or very loud tones to those who have failed to respond to His gentle touches.

The touch can come when the word is being read, when the word is being heard, at prayer or at any other time. The thing that matters is that there be communion between the Holy Spirit and the human spirit. When that communion is maintained then the human spirit will receive the slightest touch from the Holy Spirit.

The believer should protect his spirit from conditions that will make it unable to receive the touch of the Holy Spirit. Apart from sin and laziness, the human spirit that is broken, crushed, choked, and so on, may not receive the touch of God as it ought.

The Lord touched the hearts of those who were with Saul. Some went with him. Others despised him. We can say that those who responded were made willing whereas those who despised him were hardened towards him and brought him no present.

33

•••••••••

A heart hardened

When God touches the heart of a person and revels something to him, he is free to respond or to refuse to respond. When he does not respond either because of:

neglect,

laziness,

forgetfulness,

or because of a determined effort not to respond or by doing the very opposite of what God wants, the heart is hardened. Normally, a person first hardens his heart. If he continues to resist God's appeals, God may take over and harden his heart so that the heart is doubly hardened.

Pharaoh is an example of a man who received revelation from the Lord but hardened his heart and later on God hardened his heart for him. The Bible says:

1. *"Still Pharaoh's heart was hardened, and he would not listen to them; as the Lord had said"* (Exodus 7:13).
2. *"So Pharaoh's heart remained hardened, and he would not listen to them; as the Lord had said"* (Exodus 7:22).

3. *"But when Pharaoh saw that there was a respite, he hardened his heart, and would not listen to them; as the Lord had said"* (Exodus 8:15).

4. *"But Pharaoh's heart was hardened, and he would not listen to them; as the Lord had said"* (Exodus 8:19).

5. *"But Pharaoh hardened his heart this time also and would did not let the people go"* (Exodus 8:32).

6. *"But the heart of Pharaoh was hardened, and he did not let the people go"* (Exodus 9:7).

7. *"But the Lord hardened the heart of Pharaoh, and he did not listen to them, as the Lord had spoken to Moses"* (Exodus 9:12).

8. *"But when Pharaoh saw that the rain and the thunder had ceased, he sinned yet again, and hardened his heart, he and his servants. So the heart of Pharaoh was hardened, and he did not let the people go; as the Lord had spoken through Moses"* (Exodus 9:34-35).

9. *"But the Lord hardened Pharaoh's heart, and he did not let the children of Israel go"* (Exodus 10:20).

10. *"But the Lord hardened Pharaoh's heart and he would not let them go"* (Exodus 10:27).

11. *"And the Lord hardened Pharaoh's heart, and he did not let the people of Israel go out of his land"* (Exodus 11:10).

12. *"And the Lord hardened the heart of Pharaoh king of Egypt as he pursued the people of Israel as they went forth defiantly"* (Exodus 14:8).

A BELIEVER'S HEART HARDENED

A believer can harden his heart by continuing to commit a sin about which the Lord has spoken to him. He could also harden his heart by refusing to obey a command of the Lord. As far as prayer is concerned many believers harden their hearts by not responding to the gentle pressure that the Holy Spirit places on their spirits as invitation to prayer. There are times when a believer is idle and there comes a sudden urge inside him to withdraw and pray. Sometimes the subject of prayer is not revealed and the believer ought to withdraw into prayer and ask the Lord to show him what to pray about. At other times there is a clear indication of someone or some situation about which to pray. If there is no response, the heart is hardened and such touches of the Lord become rarer.

The enemy often deceives believers by telling them that they should complete what they are doing and then pray. At other times, he deceives them by telling them that they should wait for the coming pre-arranged prayer session. At other times, he sends someone or something to distract them. The believer who does not learn to obey the Lord when he calls to prayer in these unconventional ways will develop a heart that is hardened. It does not matter whether the heart is hardened as a result of deliberate sin or neglect, carelessness and distraction, the consequences are the same - the heart is hardened and there is a frustration of God's purpose.

We have learned that the only way not to harden the heart is first of all to run away from all sin or to confess and forsake sin immediately it is committed and be filled afresh with the Holy Spirit. Secondly, it is to respond immediately to the slightest touch by the Holy Spirit, inviting the believer to prayer.

Will you not repent of the sins committed against the Lord by hardening your heart? will you not do it now? If you do, the Lord will again have mercy on you and your hardened heart will be converted to a heart that is not only touched but one that is also made willing. God bless you.

34
·······

A heart willing

A heart that is willing is one that has been touched and as a result it is willing to act. Below are examples of hearts that were made willing:

1. *The Lord said to Moses, "Speak to the people of Israel, that they take me an offering; from every man whose heart makes him willing you shall receive the offering for me"* (Exodus 25:2).

2. *"And they came, every one whose heart stirred him, and every one whose spirit moved him, and brought the Lord's offering to be used for the tent of meeting, and for all its service, and for the holy garments. So they came, both men and women, all who were of a willing heart brought brooches and earrings and signet rings and armlets, all sorts of gold objects, every man dedicating an offering of gold to the Lord"* (Exodus 35:21-22).

3. *"Who then will offer willingly, consecrating himself today to the Lord?"* (1 Chronicles 29:5).

4. *"Then the people rejoiced because they had given willingly for with a whole heart they had offered freely to the Lord"* (1 Chronicles 29:9).

5. *"Tend the flock of God that is your charge, not by constraint but willingly, not for shameful gain but eagerly, not as domineering*

over those in your charge but being examples to the flock" (1 Peter 5:2-3).

A heart that is touched can become willing. However willingness of heart does not guarantee action. There are many people who are willing to do things but who nevertheless never do anything about them. There are people who are willing to pray but who do not pray. There are people who are willing to read the Bible but who nevertheless never do it. There are people who are willing to tell others about the Lord but who never get down to telling any one about the Lord.

The willing heart can be considered as a heart that has good intentions. However, good intentions are not good actions. There will be no change in your spiritual condition until you decide to translate your intentions into the Lord if someone went from door to door and actually said, *"I have come to receive an extra offering from you for the Lord. I will wait here now. So that you can give it to me."* There are many people who are willing to pray but who would not pray until someone says to them, *"Now, we are going to stop all that we are doing now and transform this hour into a prayer session."* There are many people who would not use their time well until someone tells them, *"Tomorrow, get up from sleep at four in the morning. Read the Bible from four to five o'clock. Meditate from five to six o'clock and hen go for a run of twenty minutes. After the run, ensure that you clean up, have breakfast and be at your place of work at eight o'clock."*

The fact that many people who are able to follow such a programme to their profit, are willing to do it but do not get to do it tells us that it is not enough to be willing. Something must be done to the willing heart to ensure that it satisfies the heart of God by discharging the burden that has been put on it.

When the willing heart is moved, stirred, set aglow or aflame, it will produce the action that is needed.

Let me ask you a personal question, *"Where have you stopped at being willing instead of moving into action in your relationship with the Lord?"*

Are you willing to pray? If you are for how long? When will you begin? Is there any reason why you should not begin now? I command you in the name of the Lord to put this book aside and turn to the Lord in prayer. Repent for your prayerless life. Repent for the fact that you love to read books on prayer instead of praying. Repent for the fact that you have not done anything with the truths that you have read so far in this book and of which you agreed were God's voice to you.

After you have prayed for about fifteen minutes, take out your time-table and mark out the next fifteen minutes period during which you will pray and make sure you use it for prayer. Then include on your daily time-table fifteen a minute period of praying in the morning and another in the evening. Decide that you will not have breakfast until you have prayed for the fifteen minutes. Also decide that you will not sleep until you have prayed the fifteen minutes to twenty minutes and eventually to thirty minutes. That is the way of honesty. That is the way of spiritual progress. That is the way God wants you to walk in from now on. You are willing! Praise the Lord! Let your willingness pass the test of action!!

David asked, *"Who then will offer willingly, consecrating himself today to the Lord?"* (1 Chronicles 29:5). He did not ask, *"Who then will offer willingly, consecrating himself tomorrow to the Lord?"* The willing heart moves into action today, now, and so establishes the heart in a condition of obedient action. There is no substitute to this for any who would obey. That means you!

35
•••••••••

A heart moved or stirred

A heart that is willing can move on to become a heart moved or move further on to become a heart is stirred. Below are some Bible examples:

1. *"All the women whose hearts were moved with ability spun the goat's hair"* (Exodus 35:26).

2. *"All the men and women, the people of Israel, whose heart moved them to bring anything for the work which the Lord had commanded by Moses to be done, brought it as their freewill offering to the Lord"* (Exodus 35:29).

3. *"And Moses called Bezalel and Oholiab and every and every able man in whose mind the Lord had put ability, everyone whose heart stirred him up to come to do the work"* (Exodus 36:2).

4. *"Give ear, O shepherd of Israel, thou who leadest Joseph like a flock! Thou who art enthroned upon the cherubim, shine forth before Ephraim and Benjamin and Manasseh! Stir up thy might and come to save us!"* (Psalm 80:1-2).

5. *"Yet he, being compassionate, forgave their iniquity, and did not destroy them; he restrained his anger often, and did not stir up all his wrath. He remembered that they were but flesh, a wind that passes and comes not again"* (Psalm 78:38-39).

6. *"For they provoked him to anger with their high places; they moved him to jealousy with their graven images."* (Psalm 78:58).

7. *"Have you considered my servant Job that there is none like him on the earth, a blameless and upright man who fears God and turns away from evil? He still holds his integrity, although you have moved me against him to destiny him without advise"* (Job 2:3).

8. *"In the first year of Cyrus king of Persia, that the word of the Lord by the mouth of Jeremiah might be accomplished, the Lord stirred up the spirit of Cyrus king of Persia so that he made a proclamation throughout all of his kingdom and also put it in writing: Thus says Cyrus king of Persia: The Lord, the God of heaven, has given me all the kingdoms of the earth, and he has charged me to build him a house at Jerusalem, which is in Judah"* (Ezra 1:1-2).

9. *"Then rose up the heads of the fathers' houses of Judah and Benjamin, and the priests and the Levites, everyone whose spirit God had stirred to go up to rebuild the house of the Lord which is in Jerusalem"* (Ezra 1:5).

10. *"Upright men are appalled at this, and the innocent stirs himself up against the godless"* (Job 17:8).

11. *"Bestir thyself, and awake for my right, for my cause, my God and my Lord!"* (Psalm 35:23).

12. *"And he shall stir up his power and his courage against the king of the South with a great army; and the king of the South shall wage war with an exceedingly great and mighty army; but he shall not stand, for plots shall be devised against him"* (Daniel 11:25).

13. *"But they transgressed against the God of their fathers, and played the harlot after the gods of the peoples of the land, whom God had destroyed before them. So the God of Israel stirred up*

the spirit of Pul king of Assryria, the spirit of Tilgathpilneser king of Assyria, and he carried them away" (1 Chronicles 5:25-26).

14. *"And the Lord stirred up against Jehoram the anger of the Philistines and of the Arabs who are near the Ethiopians"* (2 Chronicles 21:16).

15. *"And the Lord stirred up the spirit of Zerubbabel the son of Shealtier, governor of Judah, and the spirit of Joshua the son of Jehozadak, the high priest, and the spirit of all the remnant of the people; and they came and worked on the house of the Lord of hosts, their God"* (Haggai 1:14).

16. *"Proclaim this among the nations: Prepare war, stir up the mighty men. Let all the men of war draw near, let them come up. Beat your plowshares into swords, and your pruning hooks into spears; let the weak say, I am a warrior. Hasten and come, all you nations round about, gather yourselves there. Bring down thy warriors, O Lord. Let the nations bestir themselves, and come up to the valley of Jehosphaphat; for there I will sit to judge all the nations round about"* (Joel 3:9-12).

A HEART THAT IS WILLING NEEDS TO BE STIRRED

We have seen that a heart that is willing needs to get into action, if not its willingness will amount to nothing. The way to ensure that a willing heart does what it should do is to stir it. When a man with a burden is stirred there will be reaction. The reaction will ensure that the burden is either properly discharged or that the stirred heart becomes a heart aglow or a heart aflame which will ensure that the burden is even better taken care of. There are a number of things that need to be learned about the stirring of the heart and hearts that are stirred.

God stirs his heart

The Psalmist prayed, *"Bestir thyself, and awake for my right for my cause, my God and my Lord"* (Psalm 35:23). God can act without being stirred but when He is stirred, He acts in a greater way than He would otherwise have acted. Or, when God stirs Himself, He does what He would not have done had He not stirred up Himself.

Two things are immediately obvious: the first one is that, if God needs to stir Himself for maximum action then all believers need to stir themselves up. The second thing, that comes through is the fact that, because man can stir God to act, he should do it. The discharge of burden in prayer is really a matter of stirring God to act. The person whose burden is heavy and who is desperate to see the will of God accomplished will take no rest and give God no rest until he has stirred God up to action. God expects that serious people will *"force"* Him to act. He says, *"Upon your walls, O Jerusalem, I have set up watchmen; all the day and all the night they shall never be silent. You who put the Lord in remembrance, take no rest, and give him no rest until he establishes Jerusalem and makes it a praise in the earth"* (Isaiah 62:6-7).

God expects to be stirred

God does not just want people to pray. He wants them to imitate Him by doing all to stir Him to act. The Psalmist cried, *"Give ear, O Shepherd of Israel, thou that leadest joseph like a flock! Thou who art enthroned upon the cherubim shine forth before Ephraim and Benjamin and Manasseh! Stir up thy might and come to save us!"* (Psalm 80:1-2). The people of God are to plead with the Lord to stir Himself and come to their rescue. You

may ask, *"How can I stir the Lord up."* The answer is: God is
stirred up by

1. Asking Him to stir Himself up.

2. Importunate praying.

3. By unceasing prayer.

4. By fasting.

When a person pleads so desperately with God, putting all
that He is and all that He has into prayer, He will stir God to
action.

STIRRING GOD RESULTS IN HIS WILL BEING DONE

When a person has received the will of God by revelation
and prays it back with utmost intensity, doing all that he can
do to move God, God will allow Himself to be moved and
do what is being asked of Him. The Lord said that Satan had
moved Him against Job, *"You have moved me against him to
destroy him without cause"* (Job 2:3). If Satan is able to move
God to destruction, ought we not to move Him to salvation?
The cry, *"Stir up thy might and come to save us,"* (Psalm 80:2) can
also be *"Lord, stir up thy might and come save so-so-and-so."*

GOD STIRS THE HEARTS OF PEOPLE

What God does to Himself in stirring Himself up, He can
do in stirring the heart of someone. He stirred Cyrus and
he did what He wanted. He stirred the heads of the fathers'
houses of Judah and Benjamin, the priests and the Levites and
many others and they went to rebuild His house at Jerusalem

(Ezra 1:5). He also stirred the heart of Pul king of Assyria and he carried Israel away into captivity (1 Chronicles 5:25).

This being the case, each person with a burden ought to turn to the Lord and plead that the Lord will stir his heart, so that he will be desperate to discharge the burden that the Lord has put on His heart. When a believer sees a need but his heart is cold towards praying that the Lord would meet that need, he should plead with the Lord saying, *"Lord, my heart is cold, stir it up to pray that this need of Yours be met."* There are times when a person may have a burden but it does not weigh on him, possibly because of other things that distract him. Such a one ought to pray that the Lord should take away the things that distract him and stir him up so that he would be restless until the burden is discharged. He should also pray that he will be so stirred that there would be no rest until the maximum amount of the burden has been discharged.

We can say that a man should stir the heart of God to stir his heart to pray until the burden is discharged. We can put it this way:

1. Man has a burden.
2. Man prays that God's heart be stirred to stir his heart.
3. God hears the prayer and stirs the man's heart.
4. The man with a heart stirred prays even more that the heart of the Lord be stirred further to further stir his own heart.
5. God's heart is further stirred and consequently stirs the man's heart to the maximum.

6. The highly stirred heart of man discharges the burden to
   the maximum, thus enabling God's will to be done to the
   highest degree possible.

MAN CAN STIR UP HIS OWN HEART

We have seen that God does stir His own heart and that by
prayer man can cause God to stir up His heart. We have also
seen that God can stir up the heart of man. In addition to this,
a man can stir up his heart. A man stirs up his heart in the same
way by which he stirs the heart of the Lord, namely:

1. By asking God to do it.
2. By unceasing prayer.
3. By fasting.
4. By seeking the Lord.
5. By turning away from all unrighteousness.
6. By fixing his eyes on the Lord and on the burden that
   must be discharged.
7. By reading the Word.
8. By obeying all that he knows is the will of God.

By doing these things the person will stir his heart to
discharge the burden of the Lord.

MAN CAN STIR UP ANOTHER

Man can stir the Lord. He can stir himself. He can also stir
others. The Bible says, *"Stir up the mighty men."* A praying man
can stir the heart of another to labour to discharge the burden
of the Lord. In order to stir up another person, a praying

believer should do all that he can to stir himself up. He should in addition: encourage, exhort, challenge and do all he can to ensure that the person he wants to stir sees the vision, has the burden, protects the burden and then labours to see that it is discharged. He should also pray that the person should have the strength to carry and maintain the burden, not discharging it pre-maturely. Another thing that a person needs to pray for a person who needs to be stirred is that, God should impart faith into his heart, for hearts that are full of faith are easily stirred.

This can be done systematically in prayer. The following steps may be followed:

1. Intercession that the person will keep close to the Lord so that the burden may continue to grow.

2. Intercession that the stirred heart may not retrograde into a heart that is moved, then willing, then touched and then hardened.

3. Intercession that the burden will not be discharged pre-maturely. In prayer, block all the channels that could give way to pre-mature discharge.

4. By prayer ask the Lord to stir the heart to the maximum.

5. By prayer ask the Lord to transform the heart from one that is stirred to one that is aglow and then aflame.

6. By prayer remove any barriers that the enemy may put on to prevent the heart from being changed into one that is aglow or aflame.

PEOPLE CAN STIR THEMSELVES AND STIR OTHERS

What a person can do to stir himself and to stir another can be done by a person to stir himself, another and others. It can also be done by a group of people to stir one other person, themselves as a group and another group of people. The Bible says, *"Prepare war, stir up the mighty men"* (Joel 3:9). The Bible continues to say, *"Let the nations bestir themselves, and come to the valley of Jehoshaphat; and there I will sit to judge all the nations round about"* (Joel 3:12).

The implications of this is that one believer can stir himself, then stir another believer and even stir a multitude of believers to discharge the burden of the Lord.

This means that God has provided a way through which one believer who sees his need and has it met can then cause the needs of others to be met. This also means that a cold prayer meeting could reflect the cold and abiding condition of the leader of the meeting. It should not continue like that. He should arise, stir himself up and stir the others up. On the other hand, another believer who sees his need should seek the Lord and have it met and then while stirred, should cause the leader and the others to be stirred. This will result in an assemble of stirred people praying to the Lord and discharging His burden on their hearts.

My prayer is that you who reads this would labour to be perpetually stirred with the burden of the Lord and that you will influence multitudes to be equally stirred. Praise the Lord. Amen.

36

....

A heart aglow

When a burdened heart is stirred, three things could happen to it. First of all, it could discharge its burden at once. Secondly, the heart could be changed into one that is aglow. Thirdly, it could be changed into one that is aflame. Whether a burden would be discharged as from a heart aglow or aflame depends on the nature of the burden.

There are burdens that must be carried for a long time. Regardless of how faithful and mature the burden bearer is, he will not be able to get rid of the burden in a few hours, days, weeks and even months. Such a burden could include the evangelization, planting of Churches and entire conquest of a pagan tribe for the Lord. Such a task will take is long period of time to be accomplished. It is also important that the burden be maintained fully alive, growing and stable. It has to be prevented from pre-mature discharge.

I have seen people who were truly burdened move to a place that required years to see the Lord's victory, carried out some quick and superficial activity, and then lost their burden and left. This ought not to be so.

The answer to this is for the heart that is burdened to move from the condition of being stirred to the condition of being aglow. The Bible says, *"Never flag in zeal, be aglow with the Spirit, serve the Lord. Rejoice in your hope, be patient in tribulation, be constant in prayer"* (Romans 12:11-12). The one with a heart aglow is the one who must never flag in zeal even though it takes many months and years. That one is the one who must be patient and who must continue constantly in prayer over a long period of time.

A spirit aglow is one which is burning like big logs of wood put together. There is no flame but there is steady burning. There is no lukewarmness. There is no quick burning out. There is intense and continuous heat. The results are not spectacular overnight. Rather, there is steady fruit.

Such discharge of burden is that which is indispensable for those who must importunate. The word of God calls to importunate praying saying, *"And he told them a parable, to the effect that they ought always to pray and not lose heart. He said,"* In a certain city there was a judge who neither feared God nor regarded man; and there was a widow in that city who kept coming to him and saying, 'Vindicate me against my adversary.' For a while he refused; but afterwards he said to himself, *'Though I neither fear God nor regard man, yet because this woman bothers me, I will vindicate her, or she will wear me out by her continual coming.' "And the Lord said, Hear what the unrighteous judge says. And will not God vindicate his elect, who cry to him day and night? Will he delay long over them? I tell you, he will vindicate them speedily. Nevertheless, when the Son of man comes, will he find faith on earth?"* (Luke 18:1-8).

Let us look at a few features of the Lord's teaching: First of all, there was a disinterested judge. Secondly, the woman kept coming, to the point when he recognized that she would wear him down by her continual coming. She was patient. She was determined. She knew that she had to be vindicated regardless of how long it took. She knew that she could wear down the judge's reluctance. Thirdly, she did and was vindicated. Fourthly, the Lord is better in every way than the unrighteous judge. Nevertheless, he expects His to cry out to him day and night. Fifthly, He will vindicate those who cry out to Him day and night. The capacity to cry out to Him day and night is a manifestation of faith which may be lacking at His return. Faith keeps the praying saint burning the oil of prayer day and night. Faith refuses to accept delay or refusal. Faith presses on knowing in whom he has believed.

The aglow knows how to cry out to God. It knows desperation. Below are examples of cries to God in prayer and it is obvious that none who cried out ever went unheard.

1. *"In the course of those many days the king of Egypt died. And the people of Israel groaned under their bondage, and cried out for help, and their cry under bondage came up to God. And God heard their groaning, and God remembered his covenant with Abraham, with Isaac, and with Jacob. And God saw the people of Israel, and God knew their condition"* (Exodus 2:23-25).

2. *"And the people of Israel said to Samuel,"* Do not cease to cry to the Lord our God for us, that he may save us from the hand of the Philistines.*" So Samuel took a sucking lamb and offered it as a whole burnt offering to the Lord; and Samuel cried to the Lord for Israel, and the Lord answered him. As Samuel was offering up the burnt offering, the Philistines drew near to attack Israel; but the Lord thundered with a mighty voice that day against the Philistines and threw them into confusion; and they were routed before Isra"l"* (1 Samuel 7:8-10).

3. *"So that they caused the cry of the poor to come to him, and he heard the cry of the afflicted"* (Job 34:28).

4. *"In my distress I called upon the Lord; to my God I cried for help. From his temple he heard my voice, and my cry to him reached his ears"* (Psalm 18:6).

5. *"When the righteous cry for help, the Lord hears, and delivers them out of all their troubles"* (Psalm 34:17).

6. *"I cry to God Most High, to God who fulfils his purpose for me. He will send from heaven and saw me, he will put to shame those who trample upon me"* (Psalm 57:2-3).

The heart aglow knows how to cry to God night and day. It knows need but it also knows that the Lord will rise and answer.

37

....

Long-term goals and long-term burdens

God established an eternal purpose from eternity past. He set out a clear goal and He is steadily working to consummate it. It is taking thousands of years to accomplish that which He set out, but He nevertheless pursues His purpose. His is a long-term goal and a long-term burden. The Lord Jesus had a long-term goal. His goal was to have the Church as an eternal Bride - without spot, without wrinkle and without blemish. He set out to work this out. He was slain as a sacrifice for His Bride from the very foundations of the world. He gave Himself on the Cross to purchase His Bride. Since His ascension He fasts and prays for His Bride to be perfected. The Bible says, *"And when the hour came, he sat at table, and the apostles with him. And he said to them,"* I have earnestly desired to eat this passover with you before I suffer; for I tell you I shall not eat it again until it is fulfilled in the kingdom of God. *"And he took a cup, and when he had given thanks he said, Take this, and divide it amongst yourselves; for I tell you that from now on I shall not drink of the fruit of the vine until the kingdom of God comes"* (Luke 22:14-18). The Lord has thus been fasting from then until now, a period of one thousand nine hundred and fifty-five years. He has also been praying since then (Hebrews 7:25). So it is seen that the

Lord Jesus has long-term goals and He is aglow with the Spirit, pressing on and carrying a long-term burden until the goal is accomplished.

The Lord is seeking for people to whom He can impart revelations that will take long to accomplish. He seeks men who will keep their eyes on Him for one, two, ten and it need be, fifty years. He seeks people who will bear His burdens with Him for one, two, ten and if need be fifty years. He seeks people whose contact with Him is deep and deepening so that the fire in them will remain burning until the goal is accomplished. He seeks those who will not give up even though decades pass-by because they have seen the heavenly pattern and must build according to it. They have seen the heavenly *"tabernacle"* and are enraptured by its beauty that they must wait. They can pay the price of waiting, for what can substitute for its beauty?

If indeed you have received a long-term goal from the Lord, be aglow with the Spirit. Be aglow with the burden. The Lord will see you through to the discharge of the burden, regardless of how long it may take.

You are called by the Lord to be faithful. You must take your eyes off the others and off what they are doing for the Lord. Again I say that you are called to sustained faithfulness. The Lord says to you, *"Let your loins be girded and your lamps burning, and be like men who are waiting for their master to come home from the marriage feast, so that they may open to him at once when he comes; truly I say to you, he will gird himself and have them sit at table, and he will come and serve them. If he comes in the second watch, or in the third, and finds them so, blessed are those servants! But know this, that if the householder had known at what hour the thief was coming, he would not have left his house to be broken into. You also must be ready; for the Son of man is coming at an unexpected hour."* Peter said, *"Lord, are you telling this parable for us or for all?"* And the Lord said, *"Who then is the faithful and wise steward, whom his master will set over his household, to give them their portion of food at the proper time? Blessed is that servant whom his master when he comes will find so doing. Truly, I say to you, he will set him over all his possessions. But if that servant says to himself, 'My master is delayed in coming,' and begins to beat the menservants and the maidservants, and to eat and drink and get drunk, the master of that servant will come on a day when he does not expect him and at an hour he does not know, and will punish him, and put him with the unfaithful"* (Luke 12:35-46).

So, be faithful is carrying the burden, the sustained burden. You may yearn for the release of the burden but press on with it. You may cry out under its yoke as one believer cried:

"I count the long days, minutes, seconds that must be spent

Before Thine all-lovely face I see

Time seems to pass but the time of Thine arrival appears no nearer

When my yearning eyes will behold Thee who act the crowning joy of my being.

Does Thou know, Beloved, that I pine away out of longing for Thee?

Does Thou know that mine heart can no longer know true satisfaction

While Thou, the one ambition of its existence art away?

Won't Thou come quickly before my frame and being shatter for want of Thee?"

(Z.T.F., 1981)

Look to Him and be encouraged. He too has borne a burden for thousands of years, waiting and longing that it be discharged. He understands your agony. He understands your pain. He is not indifferent. He says, *"My son, be faithful. Press on. You have come a long way. Victory will soon be won and in exchange for your sustained burden, I will give you an eternal crown."*

May be it is time now to rise and continue to carry those prayer burdens that you gave up long ago because the answers were long in coming. Maybe you want to begin again to fast and pray for the conversion of that one for whom you had prayed for years and then given up as a hopeless case. There are no hopeless cases with God. Maybe you want to start to pray again for that backslider whom you had prayed for before and then given up because the more you prayed, the more the person plunged into sin. There is yet hope for him. Rise and continue to pray. Keep right on praying regardless of how impervious the heart of the person may appear. God is hearing you and soon there will be an answer. Listen, when the answer comes, it will be sudden. It will be fast. Praise the Lord!

38

•••••••

A heart aflame

The difference between the heart aglow and the heart aflame is that the heart aflame cannot wait while the heart aglow can wait with its burden. There is a sense in which the heart aglow can be converted into the heart aflame, when the Lord suddenly wants quick results. This demands that the praying saint walk in such intimate fellowship with the Lord that he will always know what God wants about the burden he is carrying on his heart. He must know whether the Lord desires that he continues to carry the burden or if He now wants the burden to be discharged.

If the chief characteristics of a heart that is aglow with a burden are faithfulness and perseverance, then the chief characteristics of a heart aflame are intimacy and an outpouring of spiritual fuel.

What is the secret of intimacy with the Lord? The secret of intimacy is a total response to the Lord. Those who seek Him and come to Him, crying out to Him with their whole heart will know intimacy with Him. Below are a few exhortations and testimonies of whole-heartedness:

1. And they entered into a covenant to seek the Lord, the God of their fathers, with all their heart and with all their

soul; and that whoever would not seek the Lord, the God of Israel, should be put to death, whether young or old, man or woman. They took oath to the Lord with a loud voice, and with shouting, and with trumpets, and with horns. And all Judah rejoiced over the oath; for they had sworn with all their heart, and had sought him with their whole desire, and he was found by them, and the Lord gave them rest round about" (2 Chronicles 15:12-15).

2. *"I will give thanks to the Lord with my whole heart"* (Psalm 9:1).

3. *"Praise the Lord. I will give thanks to the Lord with my whole heart, in the company of the upright, in the congregation"* (Psalm 111:1).

4. *"Blessed are those who keep his testimonies, who seek him with their whole heart"* (Psalm 119:2).

5. *"With my whole heart I seek thee; let me not wander from thy commandments!"* (Psalm 119:10).

6. *"With my whole heart I cry; answer me, O Lord! I will keep thy statutes"* (Psalm 119:145).

The total concentration and total investment of all on the Lord will ensure that there is spiritual intimacy. Then when the fire of the Lord falls on a man with a burden who is near the Lord, there will be a flame ignited and it will sweep everything in one go and the burden shall be discharged.

Those who seek God with their whole heart invest nothing away from the Lord. They look to Him but they are also prepared to fail one hundred per cent should the Lord fail. Their faith in the Lord is implicit. They do all that they must do and all that they can do and then wait on the Lord for the indispensable flame.

The story of Elijah and the prophets of Baal illustrates what we are thinking about. The Bible says *"When Ahab saw Elijah, Ahab said to him,"* Is it you, you troubler of Israel? *"And he answered,"* I have not troubled Israel; but you have, and your father's house, because you have forsaken the commandments of the Lord and followed the Baals. Now therefore send and gather all Israel to me at Mount Carmel, and the four hundred and fifty prophets of Baal and the four hundred prophets of Asherah, who eat at Jezebel's table.

So Ahab sent to all the people of Israel, and gathered the prophets together at Mount Carmel. And Elijah came near to all the people, and said, *"How long will you go limping with two different opinions? If the Lord is God, follow him; but if Ball, then follow him."* And the people did not answer him a word. Then Elijah said to the people, *"I, even I only, am left a prophet of the Lord; but Baal's prophets are four hundred and fifty men. Let two bulls be given us; and let them choose one bull for themselves, and out it in pieces and lay it on the wood, but put no fire to it; and I will prepare the other bull and lay it on the wood, and put no fire to it. And you call on the name of your god and I will call on the name of the Lord; and the God who answers by fire, he is God."* And all the people answered, *"It is well spoken"*(1 Kings 18:17-24).

"Then Elijah said to all the people, Come near to me; and all the people came near to him. And he repaired the altar of the Lord that had been thrown down; Elijah took twelve stones, according to the number of the tribes of the sons of Jacob, to whom the word of the Lord came saying, Israel shall be your name; and with the stones he built an altar in the name of the Lord. And he made a trench about the altar, as great as would contain two measures of seed. And he put the wood in order, and cut the bull in pieces and laid it on the wood. And he said, Fill four jars with water, and pour it on the burnt offering, and on the wood. And he said, Do it a second time; and they

did it a second time. And he said, Do it a third time; and they did it a third time. And the water ran round about the altar, and filled the trench also with water. And at the time of the offering of the oblation, Elijah the prophet came near and said, O Lord God of Abraham, Isaac and Israel let it be known this day that thou art God in Israel and that I am thy servant, and that I have done all these things at thy word. Answer me, O Lord, answer me, that this people may know that thou, O Lord, art God, and that thou hast turned their hearts back. Then the fire of the Lord fell, and consumed the burnt offering, and the wood, and the stones, and the dust, and licked up the water that was in the trench. And when all the people saw it, they fell on their faces; and they said, The Lord, he is God; the Lord, he is God. And Elijah said to them, Seize the prophets of Baal; let none of them escape. And they seized them; and Elijah brought them down to the brook Kishon, and killed them there" (1 Kings 18:30-40).

QUICK AND FAST ACTION

The action in this passage is quick and fast. From the time that Elijah called for the contest on Mount Carmel to the time that the contest was over was a matter of hours. Actually it was made much longer by the prophets of Baal who raved on in defeat until the time of the offering of the oblation.

The prophet had just finished talking to the Lord when the fire of the Lord fell. There was no waste of time.

THE ACTION WAS COMPLETE AND THOROUGH

The prophet had ensured that there could be no possibility of an accidental fire. He had poured water three times on the offering and the wood and dug a trench round the altar and allowed it to be filled with water. He ensured that if God answered, all the glory would go to Him. He also took the risk that if God did not answer, the failure would be obvious.

The fire fell and did a thorough job. It consumed the burnt offering; it consumed the wood. It consumed the stones and the dust and licked up the water that was in the trench.

That same day too, the prophets of Baal, all the four hundred and fifty of them were killed. They were not given an opportunity to think through the miracle and decide whether or not they would continue as prophets of Baal. The fire acted fast and the decision to kill them was taken at once and the decision applied at once.

The masses did not have many years, months, weeks or even days to know who was the Lord and they did not take long to confess what was obvious - *"The Lord, he is God; the Lord, he is God!"*

There are burdens that are not to be carried for long. when the burden matures the heart is transformed into a heart aflame and the burden is discharged at once with far-reaching consequences. Also, when a heart aflame receives a burden from the Lord, it has no alternative but to discharge it at once, to the glory of God.

WHAT TYPE OF HEAR TO HAVE?

We have seen that the Lord has some burdens that need hearts that are aglow and therefore would bear the burden faithfully for long. We have also seen that the Lord has some burdens that need to be discharged completely and at once.

The question then arises as to what type of heart the believer should have. The answer that the believer should consecrate himself to the Lord and ensure that he is in a heart condition that God can use in the way He wants. He should allow God to stir his heart and he should also stir his heart. He should also have others stir his heart. God will then produce out of the stirred heart one aglow or aflame.

There is another thing about this. The ministry of some people requires hearts that are aglow while the ministry of others requires hearts that are aflame. Each person should walk with God and as he cooperates with God, he will be given and he will develop the type of heart that he needs in order to be able to discharge the types of burdens that God will place on their hearts. What really matters is that each person should grow to know God most intimately and walk with Him in utter purity and then the Lord will fulfil His purpose concerning him. Praise the Lord.

38

· · · · · · · ·

With words known

Most of what we wrote earlier pre-supposed that the burden would be discharged with words that are known. That is, the revelation of the will of God will come as follows:

God
↓
Holy Spirit
↓
Human spirit
↓
Human mind
↓
Human mouth
↓
To God

Because that which comes from the Holy Spirit reaches the human mouth by passing through the human mind, the person who is discharging the burden, understands clearly what is being prayed through to God. This is the first and the most regularly used method for the discharge of burden.

In the discharge of burden with words that are known, the praying person should ensure that he prays all that he received back to the Lord. The problem with too many people is that they often receive more than they pray through. If, for example, the Lord should reveal to them that He wants to save ten people and consequently they should pray for the salvation of ten people, if the person should pray for the salvation of ten people then the ten people might be saved. If on the other hand, the person should decide to pray only for five people, then the chances are that perhaps only the five people who are prayed for will be saved. The praying person has failed to discharge all the burden that he received; he has failed to pray through all the revelation that he received.

There is another aspect to this. The Lord may reveal the fact that He wants to save ten people, one who is bound by unbelief, the other by anger, the third by pride, the fourth by witchcraft and so on. If the person who is praying the revelation back decides not to go into details but prefers to deal with the ten in a general way, the impact of his praying will be less than what it should be. Even in the matter of praying for each person, the details that God gives in the revelation must all be prayed back to Him for maximum effect.

This places real responsibility on the praying person. That is why we said earlier that he ought to write down the details of what he is receiving from the Lord so that as he prays them through he would ensure that all have been prayed through.

In the praying for the salvation of someone, the person praying should be in a position to ask the Lord for further revelation in order to pray better. He should be in a position to ask the Lord, *"Lord, what is standing in the way of this person coming to a saving knowledge of Your Son?"* The Lord might then show him that the problem is unbelief. He may then pray asking the Lord to set the person free from unbelief so that he might be saved. After he has prayed, he ought to be in a position to ask the Lord, *"Has all the barrier been removed?"* He may be told that all the barrier has not been removed. He should then ask the Lord, *"What must I do so that all the barrier should be removed?"* The Lord may tell him, *"In order that all the barrier should be removed, you should fast and pray."* He may then ask the Lord, *"For how long should I fast? Shall I fast alone or I should fast with another person or with other people."* If the Lord should reply that the person should fast and pray with other people, he may then ask the Lord to show him who are the people to be involved with him in the fast, for how long they are to fast and when the fast is to be begun. Asking and receiving all the details thus from the Lord and then doing what the Lord wants, will lead to the burden being discharged God's way and thus giving God the opportunity to act His own way for the accomplishment of His will.

It becomes obvious that God may not reveal all of His will from the beginning. He may reveal a part of His will and as the praying saint begins to respond to His will in prayer, more of it will be revealed. God has details about the things that He wants done which must be sought and prayed through.

In the matter of discharging the burden through words that are known, the actual words that are used are important. The Lord Jesus admonished, *"And in praying do not heap up empty phrases as the Gentiles do; for they think that they will be heard for their many words. Do not be like them, for your Father knows what you need before you ask him"* (Matthew 6:7-8).

The reality is that words are important in the discharge of burden. They are like weapons in a war. The soldier who is to make progress will ensure that he uses the weapons of words as they should be used. The success of a battle often depends upon the types of weapons used. The success of prayer may also depend upon the words used. Can you imagine a man who wants to kill a big viper but has only a small stick with which to strike it? That is the difficulty that a man may have, who has a heavy burden to discharge but cannot find the words with which to discharge it. Maybe it would help you to understand what we are saying here about the importance of words in the discharge of burden when you have tried to pray in a language that you know only a bit. You would say a bit of what you want to say but would stand frustrated because the weapon of words was not equal to the burden on your heart.

As people walk with God, they will learn gradually the words that they should use to discharge the burden on their hearts.

In addition to this, I want to add (even at the risk of being misunderstood) that as a person prays with others, he will learn how they are using words to discharge their burdens and perhaps sometimes use the words that he has learnt from others to discharge his own burden. However, this is delicate for it implies that the person will learn the words and concepts of another and *"try them out"* to see if they can be the vehicle through which to discharge his burden. If they work, he may use them. If they do not lead to release or do not fit in well, they must be rejected.

There should be room for a praying man to ask the Lord to give him the thought forms sentences, phrases and actual words that are most appropriate for the discharge of his burden. The Lord will answer such prayers. Once these are given, they seem to become a part of the person's possession to be used subsequently as the need may arise or demand.

There are situations in which the same prayer may be prayed in the same words over and over before there is complete discharge of burden. There are other situations in which the same prayer may be prayed through in the same words over and over on different occasions before the burden is discharged. Because prayer is actually a spiritual art, those who are to be involved in it must be open to spiritual experiments! Amen.

39

....

With words unknown

The discharge of burden with words unknown is praying in tongues. The Bible says, *"Therefore, he who speaks in a tongue should pray for the power to interpret. For if I pray in a tongue, my spirit prays but my mind is unfruitful. What am I to do? I will pray with the spirit and I will pray with the mind also; I will sing with the spirit and I will sing with the mind also!"* (1 Corinthians 14:13-15).

The praying in tongues is called praying with words unknown because it goes as follows: the revelation of God is given to His Holy Spirit who communicates it to the human spirit who then communicates it back to God through the instrumentality of the human mouth. The mind is not used as our intermediary between the human spirit and the human mouth:

God

↓

Holy Spirit

↓

Human spirit

↓

Human mouth

↓

To God

In this way of discharging the burden, the limitation of the human mind is left out; This means that the burden that is on the Holy Spirit which is communicated to the human spirit does not need the vehicle of the human mind before it can be released through the mouth back to God. There are many advantages that the one who in addition to being able to release his burden with words known, is also able to release the burden in tongues, has. We will mention some of them:

The first one is that one step in the communication chain is reduced. This means that the reduction or loss that is encountered as one goes from one step to the next is reduced. (Normally, there is significant loss as burden passes from the Holy Spirit to the human spirit; the extent of the loss being determined by the extent to which the spirit of the believer has developed its capacities of receptibility and the measure of its purity. The more developed and the purer the spirit, the less loss. There is also loss as the burden passes from the human spirit to the human mind. Again the degree of loss is dependent on the spirit's capacity to communicate what it has to the mind and on the mind's capacity to receive what the spirit is communicating. Again there is loss as the burden goes from mind to mouth and lastly there is loss as the burden goes from the mouth to the Lord.) The reduction of one step means that more of the burden on the mind of the Holy Spirit gets back to God.

The second advantage is that the discharge of burden with words unknown is like a second gathering of what was not carried through with the praying with the mind. Imagine that the total volume of what the will of God is that needs to be prayed through is 100. When the person prays with words known, let us say 50% of that volume is carried through to God. If there was no discharge of burden without words, that would be all that is discharged and all the rest would be lost. In the discharge of burden without words, another say, 25% of the burden may be carried through to the Lord. It is for that reason that the apostle said, *"What am I to do? I will pray with the spirit and I will pray with the mind also; I will sing with the spirit and I will sing with the mind also."* In this case, praying with the spirit compliments the praying with the mind; praying with the spirit completes the praying with the mind; praying with the spirit ensures that what was not carried through in the praying with the mind is carried through. You can think of it as someone who can *"run"* by jumping on the right leg (praying with the mind) and can also *"run"* by jumping on the left leg (praying with the spirit) but for good speed, he needs both legs (the mind and the spirit).

The third advantage is that there are some burdens on the mind of the Holy Spirit that are beyond the capacity of the human mind to understand. Such burdens cannot be discharged by the one who prays only with words known. However they can and they are able to be carried through by the one who can pray also with words unknown.

The fourth advantage is that the person who prays with words known and with words unknown can pray for a longer period and can pray over many more issues with great intensity than the person who prays with the mind only. In fact, it is like two people praying together. When one is praying with the mind, the *"system"* for praying with the spirit relaxes and is re-charged and reviewed. When the person is tired of praying with the mind, he switches to praying with the spirit. The spirit that had a break now comes in with full forces while the mind system takes its own rest, waiting to come in when the spirit would be tired. In this way there is extended praying with full vigour over a long time and this leads to more burdens or more of the same burden being brought to the Lord. This also means that the praying person is able to be released of all the burden he is carrying, faster.

Three more things need to be said here about the discharge of burden with words unknown. The first of these is that it should not be understood that when one prays with words unknown, he is praying like a robot, in which case, his mind is totally uninvolved. If that were the case, it would be dangerous, for in all conditions where the mind is rendered completely inactive, grounds are created for evil spirits to take over and govern the person. In the praying without words, the mind remains active. The only difference is that it is relieved of its function of receiving thoughts from the human spirit and converting them to human thought forms for onward communication to the mouth. All the other functions of the mind remain operative, for the person who is praying with words unknown knows what is happening and co-operates actively. The second thing that needs to be said is that, in the discharge of burden with words unknown, the will of man is fully operative. Man has to will to pray in tongues. There will be times when the switch from praying with tongues to praying with the mind is spontaneous and there will be times when the switch from praying with tongues to praying with the mind is spontaneous and there will be time when the mind has to decide that the praying is with the mind or in tongues. Finally there will be times when the whole system is exhausted but because of the intensity of the conflict, pressure has to be exerted on the praying-with-words-unknown system to continue to press on until total victory has been won. It can then be understood that the praying with words unknown is not always a pleasure. Sometimes it is very pleasurable. At other times it is a sheer burden. However, regardless of whether it is a pleasure or a burden, it must be used when it can to ensure that the purpose of God, and by His grace the purpose of man, is accomplished. The praying person is then like a soldier at the battle front. He is not looking for pleasure but for victory.

The third thing is that, the person who prays in tongues can ask and receive the gift of interpretation of tongues. In fact he is encouraged to do so. The apostle Paul exhorts, *"He who speaks in a tongue should pray for the power to interpret"* (1 Corinthians 14:13). The power to interpret operates at two levels. First of all, it can operate at the public level in which public tongues are interpreted for the benefit of the people of God. Secondly, it can operate at the personal or private level in which the person who is praying with words unknown knows what is coming through in other tongues. This is really good, for often the praying in tongues becomes directional. As he begins to pray in tongues and the interpretation is given for his mind to understand, he understands the direction in which the spirit is praying and re-aligns the mind to pray in that direction; he understands the things that the spirit is asking and then uses the mind to reinforce the request. This is able to lift prayer to very high planes.

The fourth thing that needs to be said is that, the power to pray with words unknown can be asked and received from the Lord. The apostle Paul wrote, *"Now I want you all to speak in tongues"* (1 Corinthians 14:5). You can ask the Lord to give you the Spiritual manifestation of speaking in other tongues. Ask and you will receive that your joy may be full. Praise the Lord.

40

••••••••

With sighs and groans

What happens in the discharge of burden can be illustrated as follows:

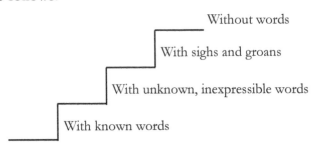

Levels of discharge of burden

A person can bear a heavy burden and go very far in discharging it through praying with words known. Some burdens are such that regardless of how the person exercises himself in praying with words known, the totality of the burden cannot be discharged without resorting to praying with words unknown. The thing about this is the fact that the person who can only pray with words known, may not know that he would have attained a higher level in the discharge of his burden if he were able to pray with words unknown, the person who is able to pray with words known and unknown may also spend his entire Christian life praying with satisfaction of those two planes without knowing that there is something more than that. That enables him to be satisfied with his prayer life provided he grows in the quality and quantity that is available at those planes. He may discharge 75% of his burden without realising that there is 25% of the burden undischarged. On the other hand it could be that for someone who can only pray at the plane of words known, God gives him only burdens that can all be discharged through total application of oneself at that plane, whereas for the person who is able to pray with words known and words unknown, God allows him to have burdens that can be completely discharged by using those two ways. I honestly do not know what the real situation is. I do not know whether God allows a person only to have burdens which can be completely discharged by total labour at the plane where one is or that he makes the one who has fully and totally exerted himself at the plane where he is to feel at ease with only a part of the burden released. From my own experience, I am only say that I was fully fulfilled by intense and extensive praying with my mind what I could not pray in tongues. However, when I was given the gift of speaking in other tongues, I found that an entirely new world of prayer was opened to me. It was most exciting. I dived into all the directions that I could at that plane. This continued for about ten years and then was suddenly introduced into the level of groans and sighs. I would start praying with words known, and then I would move into praying with words unknown and then with words known and then with words unknown. As the prayer battle intensified, I would just continue to pray with words unknown without being able then to pray with words known. Then I would be lifted to another plane where I would pray with words known, then words unknown and then sighs and groans. At that plane, things could start with intense praying with words known and then unknown and then there would be sighs and groans followed by prayer with words known or unknown and then sighs and groans. This would continue until there would be prayer only with words unknown and then sighs and groans and as the burden intensified all that would take place would be sighs and groans. At that point it is as if all of one's body is breaking and from the beginning, every sigh or groan causes the burden to grip one more and press with greater heaviness. This would go on and on to a peak and after that, each sigh or groan would cause a slight release and so on until the burden is completely gone or until that crushing burden is gone and the burden that is left is the kind that can be handled at the level of praying with words unknown. I can illustrate my experience as follows:

- Pouring our oneself without words
- Praying without words
- Pouring out oneself with groans
- Pouring out oneself with sighs and groans
- Pouring out oneself with unknown words, sighs and groans
- Pouring out oneself with known words, unknown words, sighs and groans
- Pouring out oneself with unknown words
- Pouring out oneself in prayer with known and then unknown words
- Praying intensely with known words and then unknown words
- Praying with known words and then with unknown words
- Pray with unknown words
- Pour out oneself with known words
- Pray intensely with known words
- Pray with known words

Experience in prayer at some planes.

In praying with sighs and groans, the communication is as follows:

The Lord God

↓

The Holy Spirit

↓

The Human spirit

↓

Sighs and groans

↓

The Lord God

The course is again shorter because the human mouth has to carry very little. The entire burden is concentrated in such a way that it is released through sighs and groans. Here, constructed sentences are not needed. Long phrases are not needed. Sometimes it is the ejaculation of a word or two, like the following:

"O Lord"

"O Lord"

"O, O, O Lord"

"Yes Lord!"

"Now Lord"

"O Now Lord".

At other times it may just be sighs, sighs, groans and groans.

At the beginning, it is often words known, then words unknown and then sighs and groans. As prayer deepens, the pouring out of oneself with words known ceases and all is with words unknown, sighs and groans and as the battle continues the praying with words unknown ceases and there are just sighs and groans. As this begins, there are often many sighs and groans per unit of time but then they become fewer and at some point sighs cease completely and then there continues just to be an occasional groan.

As I have earlier said, at this point in the discharge of burden the entire person - spirit, soul and body is in a state of agony, deep agony. Sometimes it is as if there is limitless pain flowing over all of a person's being. Sometimes it is as if unless the pain stopped one would die soon or almost immediately. At some point, all else is forgotten as one is lost in the agony of carrying and discharging the crushing burden. This goes on until a peak is reached and then the descent to normal begins.

THE HOLY SPIRIT IS THE AUTHOR

The praying with sighs and groans is something which must be authored by the Holy Spirit. For anyone to try and create it by any form of manipulations or imitation is to do serious harm to his whole spiritual life. A person should be satisfied to exert himself with all of his being in praying with his mind. He should ask the Lord to give him the gift of praying with words unknown and then he should wait on the Lord to do it. To try and manipulate oneself or to allow oneself to be manipulated into *"speaking in tongues"* may lead to very severe spiritual damage. No one can hoist the hand of the Holy Spirit into doing what He does not want to do or into doing what He wants to do in man's own time instead of His own. The counsel of the Psalmist on this is: *"Take delight in the Lord, and he will give you the desires of your heart. Commit your way to the Lord;*

trust in him, and he will act. He will bring forth your vindication as the light, and your right as the noonday. Be still before the Lord, and wait patiently for him" (Psalm 37:4-7). Yes, the believer should ask the Lord and cry out to Him. However, after doing that, he must wait on the Lord. Often, people want to move to the next plane before they have exhausted the possibilities that the Lord has made for them at the plane where they are. Sometimes they desire the next plane merely out of pride or out of curiosity. These have no place in the spiritual life at all, and should be rejected. I may even add that when a person is ripe for the next plane the Lord would promote him to it even though he may know nothing about it (of course those who know about it and quality for it and then ask, will receive). So the question is not so much what plane are is on but whether or not the heart of the Lord is being satisfied. We make it our aim to satisfy Him. We make that our only aim.

We have said that the Holy Spirit is the One who leads people into the various planes of prayer. As far as praying with the mind (words known) is concerned, that begins in a new and real way with the new birth and in the new birth, the Holy Spirit is the One who imparts the life of God into the heart of man. The next plane, the plane of praying with words unknown comes with the baptism into the Holy Spirit and He is the One into whom the believer is baptized by the Lord Jesus. The next plane, that of praying without words, comes with the crisis of marriage to the will of the Lord, and the plane of praying without words is the portion of people whose desire is to depart and be with the Lord which is far better. They have lived for years in the experience of being married to the will of Another, that another being the Lord Jesus. In living there, they have satisfied the heart of God unceasingly, and through many tests and trials, manifest the fact that their one desire is to depart and be with the Lord which is far better. However, they are willing, to remain in the body and serve the Lord, thus ensuring that His will is done. Being thus in that condition, the Lord would take the believer often into His immediate presence for communion and in the Lord's presence there is flow from the Lord to the believer and prayer from the believer to the Lord, that needs no words. God willing, we shall write about this in the last book in this series, *"Burning Out For God In Prayer."*

For now we say that believers can experience these various levels. The level of praying with sighs and groans is, in a special way, that of the Holy Spirit. It is His normal *"plane"* of praying and of course He enjoys all other higher planes that are not known to us. The Bible says, *"Likewise the Spirit helps us in our weakness; for we do not know how to pray as we ought, but the Spirit himself intercedes for us with sighs too keep for words. And he who searches the hearts of men knows is the mind of the Spirit, because the Spirit intercedes for the saints according to the will of God"* (Romans 8:26-2727).

The Holy Spirit is interceding. This explains many things; It explains the reason why we are receiving all that we are receiving from the Lord even in the absence of prayer or in the absence of much prayer or, in the absence of quality prayer... It explains the reason why we have kept making progress even though our prayer lives are not proportional to the great progress that we have made. It explains why desires of our hearts that we have not even transformed into prayer are granted. It explains why even the weakest saint who dares to pray constantly, continuously and aggressively can overthrow even mighty Satanic hosts in the unseen realm.

Yes, the Holy Spirit intercedes for us with sighs too deep for words. Let us praise Him and encourage Him by living lives in prayer that satisfy Him and also by exhausting all the possibilities in prayer at the plane where we are, so that by God's grace we may be promoted and one day we shall be able to pray with sighs too deep for words - pray as He prays and how glad He will be. Amen.

41
• • • • • • • •

Rending heaven - 1. God doing it.

The prophet Isaiah cried, *"O that thou wouldst rend the heavens and come down, that the mountains might quake at thy presence - as when fire kindles brushwood and the fire causes water to boil - to make thy name known, to thy adversaries, and that the nations might tremble at thy presence!"* (Isaiah 64:1-2).

This was a cry that God would come down and act. In order that He might come down, the heaven's needed to be rent. The question is, *"Who may rend the heavens?"* We answer that God is able to rend the heavens nd come down. It is as if He wants to come down but the heavens are in the way. If they are rent, He would come down. If they remain sealed, then He can't.

God is able to rend the heavens and come down and act in might but He waits to be invited to do so. He could take the initiative and do that. He has chosen to wait until He is invited - prayed into doing it. The Psalmist prayed, *"Bow thy heavens, O Lord and come down! Touch the mountains that they may smoke! Flash forth the lightning and scatter them, send out thy arrows and rout them! Stretch forth thy hand from on high, rescue me and deliver me from the many waters, from the hands of aliens, whose mouths* speak lies, and whose right hand is a right hand of falsehood" (Psalm 144:5-8).

This cry of the Psalmist that the Lord would bow the heavens and come down was answered. The Bible says, *"He bowed the heavens, and came down; thick darkness was under his feet. He rode on a cherub, and flew; he came swiftly upon the wings of the wind. He made darkness his covering around him, his canopy thick clouds dark with water. Out of the brightness before him there broke through his clouds hailstones and coals of fire. The Lord also thundered in the heavens, and the Most High uttered his voice, hailstones and coals of fire. And he sent out his arrows, and scattered them; he flashed forth lightnings, and routed them. Then the channels of the sea were seen, and the foundations of the world were laid bare, at thy rebuke, O Lord, at the blast of the breath of thy nostrils. He reached from on high, he took me, he drew me out of many waters. He delivered me from my strong enemy, and from those who hated me; for they were too mighty for me"* (Psalm 18:9-17).

The Lord is waiting that His praying people might invite Him to rend the heavens and came down to act on their behalf. He is waiting that His may cry to Him saying, *"Lord, rend the heavens and come down."*

This cry that God would rend the heavens is not just the nice words of people at ease. We say that it is a cry. It is the cry of people in a distress. It is the cry of people who know that unless God intervenes they are finished. It is the cry of people who are desperate to see God come down personally into their situation. The Psalmist could cry out that way because his enemies were too mighty for him.

If a person can solve his problem by any other method, then he need not plead with God to rend the heavens and come don. If some action by the Lord from a distance would do, one need bother to ask God to rend the heavens and come down, for that kind of praying demands that a man put in his all. However, if a man must, he will pay the price, cry out to God and the Lord would come down.

It is always wonderful when the Lord rends the heavens and comes down. Things are not quite the same after that. In an incident when the Lord came down, the Bible says, *"On the morning of the third day there were thunders and lightnings, and a thick cloud upon the mountain, and a very loud trumpet blast, so that all the people who were in the camp trembled. Then Moses brought the people out of the camp to meet God; and they took their stand at the foot of the mountain. And Mount Sinai was wrapped in smoke, because the Lord descended upon it in fire; and the smoke of it went up like the smoke of a kiln, and the whole mountain quaked greatly. And as the sound of the trumpet grew louder and louder, Moses spoke, and God answered him in thunder. And the Lord came down upon Mount Sinai, to the top of the mountain; and the Lord called Moses to the top of the mountain, and Moses went up"* (Exodus 19:16-20). This was followed by the Lord proclaiming the ten commandments.

Yes, it is a great event when the Lord comes down. He came down upon the disciples in the Upper Room and the Church was born.

O that some would cause Him, by their prayers, to rend the heavens and come down and let a new day begin for His people! Will you not pay the price for it? Will you not ask Him to do it? Will you not ask Him now? Will you not continue to ask Him until He has rent the heavens and come down? May the Lord help you to do it. Amen.

42

········

Rending heaven - 2. man doing it.

THE LORD JESUS RENDS THE HEAVENS

In the last chapter, we showed that God rends the heavens. We also showed that God can rend the heavens at the request of man; that God can rend the heavens in answer to prayer. In addition to man pleading with God to rend the heavens, man can rend the heavens directly. The Lord Jesus did it on at least two occasions. The Bible says, *"Now when all the people were baptized, and when Jesus also had been baptized and was praying, the heaven was opened, and the Holy Spirit descended upon him in bodily form, as a dove, and a voice came from heaven, Thou art my beloved Son, with thee I am well pleased"* (Luke 3:21-22).

There were many people who were baptized and went away rejoicing. However, when Jesus was baptized, He did not go away as the others did. He followed His baptism with prayer. So mighty, strong and penetrating was His prayer that it ascended to the heavens and rent the heavens. The heavens were thus open. Being thus open, the Holy Spirit who was waiting to descend had an open way and came upon Him in the bodily form of a dove.

This was followed by the voice of the Father that penetrated through the rent heavens and came right to earth where it was heard. Had Jesus not prayed, the heavens would have remained sealed. The dove would not have descended and the Father's voice would not have been heard!

On another occasion the Bible says, *"Now about eight days after these sayings he took with him Peter and John and James, and went up on the mountain to pray. And as he was praying, the appearance of his countenance was altered, and his raiment became dazzling white. And behold, two men talked with him, Moses and Elijah, who appeared in glory and spoke of his departure, which he was to accomplish at Jerusalem. Now Peter and those who were with him were heavy with sleep, and when they wakened they saw his glory and the two men who stood with him. And as the men were parting from him, Peter said to Jesus, Master, it is well that we are here; let us make three booths, one for you and one for Moses and one for Elijah - not knowing what he said. As he said this, a cloud came and overshadowed them; and they were afraid as they entered the cloud. And a voice came out of the cloud, saying, This is my Son, my chosen; listen to him!"* (Luke 9:28-35).

Until the Lord Jesus prayed, the heavens were sealed. However, when he prayed, He rent the heavens and thus rending of the heavens resulted in a number of things. First of all, Moses and Elijah were sent to Him to speak to Him about His coming departure. Secondly, some of the glory that was His in heaven came upon Him and caused the appearance of His countenance to be altered, and His raiment to become dazzling white. Thirdly, the voice of the Father was heard.

None of these things would have happened without the Lord Jesus rending heaven by His prayers.

YOU TOO CAN REND THE HEAVENS

What the Lord Jesus did in rending the heavens is possible for His followers. You too can rend the heavens; If the will of God becomes such a burden to you that you must see God answer in an unusual way, you will not be content to pray ordinarily. You should put all of yourself out in prayer. You should break through every barrier and if the heavens stand between you and God's intervention, you would not spare them but smash them and tear them off by your prayers and then the Lord's intervention would come.

PERSISTENCE

Those who want to rend the heavens must bear one thing in mind. The heavens are not easily rent. They do not yield to weak prayer blows. They only yield to the mighty pressures of strong prayers. In addition to violent praying, the heavens often do not give way to the first blows that they receive. They are quite resistant. Only those who are prepared to knock with all their might and keep knocking with all their might until they give way will succeed. The Bible says, *"Upon your walls, O Jerusalem, I have set watchmen; all the day and all the night they shall never be silent. You who put the Lord in remembrance, take no rest, and give him no rest, until he establishes Jerusalem and makes it a praise in the earth"* (Isaiah 62:6-7).

If you would succeed, you must keep at violent praying all the day and all the night. You must refuse to be silent. You must give God no rest. You must take no rest until the Lord has come through and given you the desire of your heart.

Is now not the time to act? I believe it is. Rise and begin to knock at the heavens with persistent violence and some day the victory will come. Praise the Lord!

43

········

Conflict with the enemy

In the discharge of burden, there are times when it is so difficult to talk to the Father. The revelation has been received, the burden has been imparted and the heart is willing, moved, stirred, aglow or aflame and yet there is a *"feeling"* that one cannot get through to God. There are times when one is tired and therefore it is difficult to discharge the burden in prayer. In the incapacity or the difficulty in discharging the burden may be the result of tiredness. However, there are other times when one is quite fresh and ready but there is no way of getting through. The burden is there and the willingness to discharge it is there but one does not seem to plug into the Lord so as to discharge the burden.

I have come to find that the devil sometimes stands in the way, blocking communication with God or causing a cloud between the burdened saint and the Lord so that there is no way to carry the burden through to God.

What is the answer to that kind of situation? It is simple. Just rebuke the devil in the name of the Lord Jesus and command6 that he should go away and stand between you and your heavenly Father no more. He will obey and things will become so clear and contact with the Father so real that the discharge of the burden will be smooth and thorough.

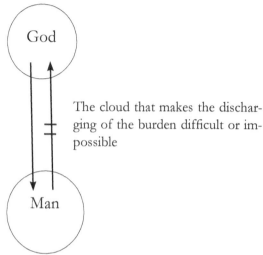

Satanic opposition to the discharging or unloading of the burden

There are times when the enemy will withdraw at a simple command in the name of the Lord Jesus. There are other times when he will not depart immediately he is told to do so and would have to be evicted from the position of interference by insisting that he leaves. Whatever is the case, any one who senses that the enemy is standing in the way should ensure that he leaves before the burden is poured out to the Lord. It is always easy to know when he has been evicted for what stood like a wall between the believer and his God or what stood like a cloud will go away and things will be so clear and communication so obvious.

44

· · · · · · · ·

No more burden

When all the burden has been successfully discharged on the Father, that is, when all of God's will that was received by revelation has been prayed back to the Father, the praying person will have no more burden. He will feel as if a heavy weight has been lifted off him. Everyone should pray for whatever he is praying for until he experiences the total release of burden. Then he should stop for God has heard him. Hannah knew what it was to be burdened, have a discharge of burden and have no more burden.

At the climax of her burden she said to Eli the high priest, *"My lord, I am a woman sorely troubled; I have drunk neither wine nor strong drink, but I have been pouring out my soul before the Lord. Do not regard your maidservant as a base woman, for all along I have been speaking out of my great anxiety and vexation"* (1 Samuel 1:15-16).

She had poured out all of her burden to the Lord. She had no more burden to pour out. The high priest gave her a word of exhortation, *"Go in peace, and the God of Israel grant your petition which you have made to him"* (1 Samuel 1:17). Those words sealed her assurance. She sealed her faith in the fact that she believed God had heard her by saying, *"Let your maidservant find favour in your eyes"* (1 Samuel 1:18). It was a kind of saying, *"Amen"* to what the high priest had said.

Because her burden was discharged, the Bible testified, *"Then the woman went her way and ate, and her countenance was no longer sad"* (1 Samuel 1:18).

WHAT SHOULD HAPPEN BETWEEN THE TIME WHEN THE BURDEN HAS BEEN COMPLETELY DISCHARGED AND THE TIME WHEN GOD'S ANSWER IS MADE VISIBLE?

The first thing is praise and thanksgiving

The second thing is praise and thanksgiving

The third thing is praise and thanksgiving

The last thing is praise and thanksgiving.

Amen.

HOW LONG WILL IT TAKE FOR THE ANSWER TO BECOME VISIBLE?

I do not know.

God alone knows.

One thing we know is that His answer will be on time. God is always on time. Let us praise Him. Amen.

1. With Christ In The School And Ministry of Prayer.
2. Knowing The Will of God.
3. The Hebrew-Greek Key Study Bible compiled by Spiros Zodhiates, Baker Book House, Grand Rapids, Michigan 49506.

4. For a fuller treatment of the subject, see our book, *"The Spirit of Man."*

5. For a fuller treatment of the subject matter in this chapter, see our book, *"Knowing the Will of God."*

6. Some tiredness and sleep is from the enemy. The answer to such is to command him to go away with his blockages.

Very important

If you have not yet received Jesus as your Lord and Saviour, I encourage you to receive Him. Here are some steps to help you,

ADMIT that you are a sinner by nature and by practice and that on your own you are without hope. Tell God you have personally sinned against Him in your thoughts, words and deeds. Confess your sins to Him, one after another in a sincere prayer. Do not leave out any sins that you can remember. Truly turn from your sinful ways and abandon them. If you stole, steal no more. If you have been committing adultery or fornication, stop it. God will not forgive you if you have no desire to stop sinning in all areas of your life, but if you are sincere, He will give you the power to stop sinning.

BELIEVE that Jesus Christ, who is God's Son, is the only Way, the only Truth and the only Life. Jesus said, «*I am the way, the truth and the life; no one comes to the Father, but by me*» (John 14:6). The Bible says, «*For there is one God, and there is one mediator between God and men, the man Christ Jesus, who gave himself as a ransom for all*» (1 Timothy 2:5-6). «*And there is salvation in no one else (apart from Jesus), for there is no other name under heaven given among men by which we must be saved*» (Acts 4:12). «*But to all who received him, who believed in his name, he gave power to become children of God...*» (John 1:12). But,

CONSIDER the cost of following Him. Jesus said that all who follow Him must deny themselves, and this includes selfish financial, social and other interests. He also wants His followers to take up their crosses and follow Him. Are you prepared to abandon your own interests daily for those of Christ? Are you prepared to be led in a new direction by Him? Are you prepared to suffer for Him and die for Him if need be? Jesus will have nothing to do with half-hearted people. His demands are total. He will only receive and forgive those who are prepared to follow Him AT ANY COST. Think about it and count the cost. If you are prepared to follow Him, come what may, then there is something to do.

INVITE Jesus to come into your heart and life. He says, *«Behold I stand at the door and knock. If anyone hears my voice and opens the door (to his heart and life), I will come in to him and eat with him, and he with me «* (Revelation 3:20). Why don't you pray a prayer like the following one or one of your own construction as the Holy Spirit leads ?

> «Lord Jesus, I am a wretched, lost sinner who has sinned in thought, word and deed. Forgive all my sins and cleanse me. Receive me, Saviour and transform me into a child of God. Come into my heart now and give me eternal life right now. I will follow you at all costs, trusting the Holy Spirit to give me all the power I need.»

When you pray this prayer sincerely, Jesus answers at once

and justifies you before God and makes you His child.

Please write to me and I will pray for you and help you as you go on with Jesus Christ...

If you have received the Lord Jesus-Christ after reading this book, please write to us at the following addresse :

For Europe :
Editions du Livre Chrétien
4, Rue du Révérend Père Cloarec
92400 Courbevoie
Courriel : editionlivrechretien@gmail.com

TRUE CONVERSION
(MARK 10:17-31)

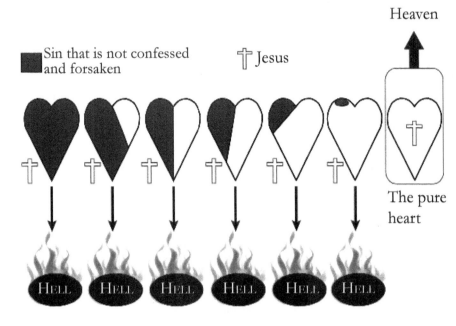

All the blemished hearts represent unsaved persons. The last pure heart alone represents the saved person.

Jesus cannot come in to blot out some of a person's sins and not others. He comes in to blot out all sins or no sin at all.

He blots out sin that is confessed and forsaken forever.

He comes in to be Saviour, Lord and King in all things and in all circumstances or He does not come in at all.

He cannot come in to be Saviour without being Lord and King because He cannot divide Himself. He is Saviour, Lord and King of all or Saviour, Lord and King of nothing at all.

Professor Zacharias Tanee Fomum

About the author

Professor Z.T. Fomum was born in 1945 in Cameroon and was taken to be with the Lord on the 14th March 2009. He was admitted to the Bachelor of Science degree, graduating as a prize-winning student from Fourah Bay College in the University of Sierra Leone. His research in Organic Chemistry earned him a Ph.D. degree in the University of Makerere, Kampala, Uganda. Recently, his published scientific work was evaluated and found to be of high distinction, earning him the award of a Doctor of Science degree from the University of Durham in Great Britain. As a Professor of Organic Chemistry in the University of Yaoundé I, Cameroon, he supervised and co-supervised more than 100 Master's and Doctoral degree theses. He published with others over 160 scientific articles in leading international journals.

The author read over 1350 books on the Christian Faith and wrote over 150 titles to advance the Gospel of Christ. 4 million copies of these books are in circulation in 11 languages, as well as 16 million gospel tracts in 17 languages. In pursuance of the purpose to proclaim the Gospel of Jesus Christ, he also made a total of over 700 missionary journeys in Cameroon and over 500 in 70 nations. These ranged from 2 days to 6 weeks in all the world's six continents.

The author led a Church-planting and missionary-sending movement, by whose ministrations, more than 10,000 healing miracles were performed by God in answer to prayer in the name of Jesus. These miracles include instant healings of; headaches, cancers, HIV/AIDS, blindness, deafness, dumbness, paralysis, madness and diverse diseases.

The author was married to Prisca Zei Fomum and they had 7 children who are all actively involved in serving the Lord. Prisca is a national and international minister specialising in the winning and discipling of children to Jesus Christ. She also communicates and imparts the vision of the ministry to children, with a view to raise and build up ministers for them.

The author owed all that he was and all that God had done in him and through him, to the unmerited favours and blessings of God and to his world wide army of friends and co-workers. He considered himself nothing without them and the blessings of God, and would have amounted to nothing but for them.

May the Lord receive all the glory!

OTHERS BOOKS BY
ZACHARIAS TANEE FOMUM

- THE CHRISTIAN WAY
- The way of life
- The way of obedience
- The way of discipleship
- The way of sanctification
- The way of Christian character
- The way of spiritual power
- The way of Christian service
- The way of spiritual warfare
- The way of overcomers
- The way of suffering for Christ
- The way of spiritual encouragement
- The way of loving the Lord
- The way of victorious praying
-

- THE PRAYER
- The ministry of fasting
- The art of intercession
- The practice of intercession
- Praying with power
- Practical spiritual warfare through prayer
- Moving God through prayer
- The ministry of praise and thanksgiving
- Waiting on the Lord in prayer
- The ministry of supplication
- Life-changing thoughts on prayer, Vol 1
- Life-changing thoughts on prayer, Vol 2
- Life-changing thoughts on prayer, Vol 3
- The centrality of prayer
-

- PRACTICAL HELPS FOR OVERCO-
MERS
- The use of time
- Retreats for spiritual progress
- Personal spiritual revival
- Daily dynamic encounters with God
- The school of truth
- How to succeed in the Christian life

- The Christian and money
- Deliverance from the sin of laziness
- The art of working hard
- Knowing God – The greatest need of the hour
- Restitution : An important message for the overcomers
- Revelation a must
- True repentance
- You can receive a pure heart today
- You can lead someone to the Lord Jesus today
- The overcomer as a servant of man
- You have a talent!
- The Making of Disciples
- The secret of spiritual fruitfulness
- The dignity of manual labour
-

- GOD, SEX AND YOU
- Enjoying the premarital life
- Enjoying the choice of your marriage partner
- Enjoying the married life
- Divorce and remarriage
- A successful marriage; the husband's making
- A successful marriage; the wife's making
-

- EVANGELISATION
- God's love and forgiveness
- Come back home my son; I still love you
- Jesus loves you and wants to heal you
- Come and see; Jesus has not changed!
- 36 reasons for winning the lost to Christ
- Soul winning, Volume 1
- Soulwinning, Volume 2
- Celebrity a mask
-

- **MAKING SPIRITUAL PROGRESS**
- Vision, burden, action
- The ministers and the ministry of the new covenant
- The cross in the life and ministry of the believer
- Knowing the God of unparalleled goodness
- Brokenness, the secret of spiritual overflow
- The secret of spiritual rest
- Making spiritual progress, Volume 1
- Making spiritual progress, Volume 2
- Making spiritual progress, Volume 3
- Making spiritual progress, Volume 4
-

- **PRACTICAL HELPS IN SANCTIFICATION**
- Deliverance from sin
- Sanctified and consecrated for spiritual ministry
- The Sower, the seed and the hearts of men
- Freedom from the sin of adultery and fornication
- The sin before you may lead to immediate death: Do not commit it!
- Be filled with the Holy Spirit
- The power of the Holy Spirit in the winning of the lost
-

- **OTHER BOOKS**
- Are you still a disciple of the Lord Jesus?
- A broken vessel
- The joy of begging to belong to the Lord Jesus : A testimony
- Laws of spiritual success, Volume 1
- Discipleship at any cost
- The shepherd and the flock
- Spiritual aggressiveness
- The secluded worshipper
- Deliverance from demons
- Inner healing
- No failure needs to be final
- You can receive the baptism into the Holy Spirit now
- Facing life's problems victoriously
- A word to the students

- The prophecy of the overthrow of the satanic prince of Cameroon
- The power to operate miracles
-

- **NEW BOOKS**
- Church Planting Strategies
- Delivrance from the Sin Of The Gluttony
- God Centredness
- God, Money And You
- In The Crucible For Service
- Issues Of The Heart
- Jesus Saves And Heals Today
- Leading A Local Church
- Meet The Liberator
- Power For Service
- Prayer And A Walk With God
- Prayer crusade Volume 1
- Revolutionary Thoughts On Spiritual Leadership
- Roots And Destinies
- Spiritual Fragrange
- Spiritual Gifts
- Spiritual Nobility
- The Art Of Worship
- The Believer's Conscience
- The Character And Personality Of The Leader
- The Leader & His God
- The Overthrow Of Principalities And Powers
- The Processes Of Faith
- The Spirit Filled Life
- Victorious Dispositions
- Walking With God
- Women Of The Glory Vol 1
- Women Of The Glory Vol 2
- Women Of The Glory Vol 3
- You, Your Team And Your Ministry

Imprimé en France par CPI
en septembre 2019

Dépôt légal : septembre 2019
N° d'impression : 154149